NATIVE DESIGNS FROM INDIA

Research & concept: Maarten Hesselt van Dinter

Editor: Mark Poysden
Italian: Valeria Scimia
French: Annabel Baltus
German: Lilian Unger
Spanish: Montserrat Sonia Pérez Rodríguez
Design & layout: Inkahootz Amsterdam, www.inkahootz.nl

Also available in the same series by HvD-Publishing:
Anche disponibile nella stessa serie di HvD-Publishing:
Ainsi disponible dans la même série de HvD-Publishing:
In der gleichen Reihe von HvD-Publishing ebenfalls erhältlich:
También está disponible en la misma serie de la editorial HvD-Publishing:

Native Designs from Ancient Mexico & Peru
Native Designs from North America
Native Designs from Indonesia
Native Designs from the Pacific

www.hvd-publishing.com

ISBN-10: 90-810543-6-8
ISBN-13: 978-90-810543-6-2
NUR: 656


info@hvd-publishing.com

Printed in China by SC (sang choy) International Ltd.

# NATIVE DESIGNS FROM INDIA

## Maarten Hesselt van Dinter

HvD Publishing

# Native Designs from India

The beautiful designs in this book are mostly geometric depictions of animals, flowers, objects and deities and are embroidered in cloths, painted on walls and ceramics, drawn on floors as talismans and even used as henna- and tattoo designs. They reflect the vitality of the Indian people, their culture and their beliefs.

The designs are strongly linked to Hinduism and Buddhism. The snake (naga), for example, is a supporter of the Hindu god Vishnu, the protector of creation and the Buddha. Nagas frequently appear as guardians around doorways to Hindu and Buddhist shrines. The elephant, regarded as lucky and sacred in India, symbolises wealth and the god Ganesh. Lotus blossoms, fish, peacocks, triangles and swastikas are symbols of happiness and protection in both religions. The lotus goddess is called Lakshmi or Lakshmi-Padma (White Lotus), the goddess of wealth and fortune, power and beauty. In Buddhism an open blossom signifies Enlightenment. The colour is important too. A pink lotus blossom is associated with the Great Buddha; a white lotus blossom signifies purity. In Bengal, for example, it was not uncommon for a Brahman, a member of the elite priestly caste, to refuse water from a girl who did not have a lotus blossom tattooed on her forehead.

Many of the complex designs represent religious symbols and are drawn as endless knots. In Buddhism, an endless knot represents Buddha's infinite wisdom and the union of compassion and wisdom. In Tamil tradition and religion, these designs are drawn on houses and near places of worship. These signs welcome people and gods into homes, especially Lakshmi, the goddess of prosperity. They are called kolam designs and are drawn by women each morning on the pavement outside the entrances to their homes. According to tradition, the lines must be completed to prevent evil spirits from entering the pattern. kolam designs are usually made with dried rice, flour or chalk but today paint is also used. The patterns can be very complicated and vary in size; during festival months, temples are decorated with patterns that cover thousands of square feet. Symmetrical patterns created with coloured sand or flour are called rangoli. Not long ago women of different castes and tribes in Tamil-Nadu tattooed these labyrinth patterns on their bodies to ensure their entry to heaven, and once there, that she was recognisable to her ancestors or her dead husband. Tattoo designs are generally used to enhance a girl's beauty; they are her personal jewellery but also function as talismans. A dot, for example, is a common specific against the evil eye, and depictions of scorpions, snakes, bees or spiders offer magical defence against bites and stings from these creatures. They also bring good fortune in marriage, life and the hereafter.

# Arts décoratifs populaires d'Inde

Les magnifiques illustrations de ce livre sont surtout des représentations géométriques d'animaux, de fleurs, d'objets et de divinités et elles sont brodées sur les tissus, peintes sur les murs et sur la céramique, dessinées sur les sols comme talismans et même utilisées comme dessins pour henné et tatouages. Elles reflètent la vitalité des indiens, leur culture et leurs convictions.

Les représentations sont fortement liées à l'hindouisme et au bouddhisme. Le serpent (naga), par exemple, est un partisan du dieu hindou Vishnu, le protecteur de la création et le Bouddha. Les Nagas apparaissent fréquemment comme gardiens aux embrasures des sanctuaires hindous et  bouddhistes. L'éléphant, considéré comme chanceux et sacré en Inde, symbolise la richesse et le dieu Ganesh. Les fleurs de Lotus, le poisson, les paons, les triangles et les svastikas sont des symboles de bonheur et de protection dans les deux religions. La déesse du lotus est appelée Lakshmi ou Lakshmi-Padma (Lotus Blanc), la déesse de la richesse et de la bonne fortune, du pouvoir et de la beauté. Dans le bouddhisme une fleur ouverte signifie l'Illumination. La couleur est également importante. Une fleur de lotus rose est associée au Grand Bouddha; une fleur de lotus blanche signifie la pureté. Au Bengale, par exemple, il n'est pas rare pour un brahmane, membre de l'élite de la caste des prêtres, de refuser de l'eau à une fille qui n'a pas de tatouage de fleur de lotus sur son front.

Beaucoup de figures complexes représentent des symboles religieux et sont dessinées en noeuds interminables. Dans le bouddhisme, un noeud sans fin représente l'infinie sagesse de Bouddha et l'union de la compassion et de la sagesse. Dans la tradition et la religion Tamoules, cependant, ces figures sont dessinées sur les maisons et près des lieux de culte. Ces signes accueillent les gens et les dieux ,  bienvenus dans les maisons, surtout Lakshmi, la déesse de la prospérité. Ils sont appelés les dessins de Kolam et sont dessinés par les femmes chaque matin sur le trottoir à l'entrée de leurs maisons. Selon la tradition, les lignes doivent être complétées afin d'empêcher les esprits diaboliques de pénétrer dans le modèle. Les dessins de Kolam sont en général réalisés  avec du riz séché, de la farine ou de la craie mais aujourd'hui la peinture est aussi utilisée. Les modèles peuvent être très compliqués et varier en taille;  pendant les mois de festival, les temples sont décorés avec des modèles couvrant des milliers de mètres carrés. Les modèles symétriques créés avec du sable ou de la farine colorée sont appelés rangoli. Il y a peu de temps encore les femmes de différentes castes ou tribus du  Tamoul-Nadu tatouaient ces modèles de labyrinthe sur leur corps pour assurer leur entrée au paradis, et une fois là-bas, pour être reconnue de leurs ancêtres ou de leur mari défunt. Les différents tatouages sont généralement utilisés pour rehausser la beauté des filles; ils sont ses bijoux personnels mais jouent aussi le rôle de talismans. Un point, par exemple, est une protection contre l'oeil diabolique, et les représentations de scorpions, de serpents, d'abeilles ou d'araignées offrent une défense magique contre les morsures et les piqûres de ces créatures. Ils amènent aussi la bonne fortune dans le mariage, la vie et l'après vie.

# Eingeborenen-Designs aus Indien

Die schönen Entwürfe in diesem Buch sind größtenteils geometrische Darstellungen von Tieren, Blumen, Objekten und Gottheiten und sind auf Tücher gestickt, auf Wände und Keramik gemalt, als Talisman auf den Boden gezeichnet und sogar verwendet als Henna- und Tattoo-Designs. Sie reflektieren die Lebenskraft der indischen Bevölkerung, ihre Kultur und ihren Glauben.

Die Entwürfe sind stark mit dem Hinduismus und Buddhismus verknüpft. Die Schlange (Naga), zum Beispiel, ist eine Stütze des Hindu Gott Vishnu, der Beschützer der Schöpfung und von Buddha. Nagas erscheinen häufig als Wächter an Zugängen zu hinduistischen und buddhistischen Schreinen. Der Elefant, in Indien als glücklich und heilig geehrt, symbolisiert Reichtum und den Gott Ganesh. Lotusblüten, Fische, Pfauen, Dreiecke und Swastikas (Sonnenräder) sind Symbole für Glück und Schutz in beiden Religionen. Die Lotus-Göttin wird Lakshmi oder Lakshmi-Padma (Weißer Lotus) genannt, die Göttin von Reichtum und Vermögen, Kraft und Schönheit. Im Buddhismus bedeutet eine offene Blüte die Erleuchtung. Auch die Farbe ist maßgeblich. Eine rosafarbene Lotusblüte wird mit dem Großen Buddha assoziiert; eine weiße Lotus-Blüte bedeutet Reinheit. In Bengal zum Beispiel war es nicht ungewöhnlich für einen Brahmanen, ein Mitglied der elitären Priester-Kaste, Wasser von einem Mädchen abzulehnen, welches keine Lotusblüte auf ihrer Stirn tätowiert hatte.

Viele dieser aufwendigen Entwürfe stellen religiöse Symbole dar und sind als endlose Knoten gezeichnet. Im Buddhismus repräsentiert ein endloser Knoten die unendliche Weisheit von Buddha und die Vereinigung von Mitleid und Weisheit. In Tradition und Religion der Tamilen hingegen, sind diese Entwürfe an Häuser gezeichnet und in der Nähe von Orten der Verehrung. Diese Zeichen heißen Menschen und Götter zu Hause willkommen, besonders Lakshmi, die Göttin des Wohlstands. Sie werden Kolam-Designs genannt und jeden Morgen von den Frauen auf den Straßenbelag außerhalb der Eingänge ihrer Häuser gezeichnet. Gemäß der Tradition müssen die Linien vollendet werden, um das Eindringen böser Geister in das Musters zu verhindern. Kolam-Designs werden im Allgemeinen aus getrocknetem Reis, Mehl oder Kreide angefertigt, aber heutzutage wird dazu auch Farbe benutzt. Die Muster können sehr kompliziert ausfallen und in ihrer Größe variieren; während der Fest-Monate, sind Tempel mit Mustern dekoriert, die Tausende von Quadratmetern bedecken. Symmetrische Muster, die mit farbigem Sand oder Mehl erstellt werden, werden Rangoli genannt. Vor nicht allzu langer Zeit tätowierten Frauen verschiedener Kasten und Stämme in Tamil-Nadu diese Labyrinthmuster auf ihre Körper, um ihren Zugang in den Himmel zu sichern, und dort angelangt, erkennbar für ihren Vorfahren oder ihren toten Ehemann zu sein. Tätowierungen werden gewöhnlich benutzt, die Schönheit eines Mädchens zu verstärken; sie sind ihr persönlicher Schmuck aber fungieren auch als Talismans. Ein Punkt zum Beispiel, ist ein geläufiges Mittel gegen den bösen Blick, und Darstellungen von Skorpionen, Schlangen, Bienen oder Spinnen bieten einen magischen Schutz gegen die Bisse und Stiche dieser Kreaturen. Sie bringen auch Glück in der Ehe, im Leben sowie dem Jenseits.

Bitte benutzen Sie diese Darstellungen frei nach Ihrem Bedarf und als eine Quelle der Inspiration. Kontaktieren Sie jedoch bitte den Herausgeber bezüglich der Erlaubnis und Gebühren für Werbezwecke, sowie für anderweitige berufliche und gewerbliche Verwendung: info@hvd-publishing.com.

## Diseños nativos de India

Los diseños de tatuajes que presentamos en este libro son descripciones geométricas en su mayoría de animales, flores, objetos. Se bordaban sobre las telas y, se pintaban en las paredes y en la cerámica. Estas tribus, utilizaban los suelos como talismanes. Estos diseños reflejan la vitalidad de los indios así como a su cultura y sus creencias.

Los diseños están ligados totalmente a hinduismo y budismo. La serpiente (naga), por ejemplo, es un partidario del Dios Vishnu hindú, protector de la creación y el Buda. Nagas aparece con frecuencia como guardianes alrededor de puertas hindúes y relicarios budistas. El elefante, considerado como afortunado y sagrado en India, es símbolo de la riqueza y del Dios Ganesh. Las flores del loto, el pez, los pavos reales, los triángulos y las esvásticas, son los símbolos de la felicidad y la protección en ambas religiones. La diosa del loto se llama Lakshmi o Lakshmi-Padma (Loto Blanco), la diosa de la riqueza y la fortuna, el poder y la belleza. En el budismo existe la creencia de que una flor abierta significa Siglo de Luces. El color es importante también. Una flor rosa del loto, se asocia con el Gran Buda; una flor blanca de loto significa la pureza. En bengala, por ejemplo, no era raro para un brahmán, un miembro de la élite de la casta de los sacerdotes, se negara a dar agua a una chica que no tuviera una flor de loto tatuada en la frente.

Muchos de los diseños complejos representan los símbolos religiosos y se dibujan nudos de manera que pareciran interminables. En budismo, un nudo interminable representa la sabiduría infinita de Buda y la unión de la compasión y la sabiduría. En la tradición y la religión Tamiles, sin embargo, estos diseños se utilizan en las casas y lugares de culto cercano. Estos signos personas bienvenidos y Dioses en hogares, especialmente Lakshmi, la diosa de la prosperidad. Ellos son llamados Kolam los diseños y son dibujados por mujeres cada mañana en el pavimento fuera de las entradas a sus hogares. Según la tradición, las líneas se deben completar para prevenir que los espíritus malos entraran en los hogares. Los diseños de Kolam se hacen generalmente con arroz seco, la harina o cretáceo pero hoy día se utiliza también la pintura. Las pautas para diseñar se pueden complicar mucho y también pueder presentar variación en el tamaño; Durante meses de festividad, los templos se decoran con los diseños que cubren millares de pies cuadrados. Las pautas simétricas que colorean la arena o la harina se llaman rangoli. No hace mucho tiempo atrás, las mujeres de castas y tribus diferentes en el Tamil-Nadu practicaban estas pautas tatuajes de laberinto en sus propios cuerpos para asegurar su entrada al cielo, y una vez que allí, ella era reconocida a por sus antepasados o por su difunto marido. Los diseños del tatuaje se utilizaban generalmente con la finalidad de aumentar la belleza de las chicas; estos tatuajes eran utilizados como su joyería personal pero también tenían la función de talismanes. Un ejemplo muy común y específico era su uso contra el mal de ojo, y contra los ataques de escorpiones, serpientes, abejas o incluso arañas. De esta manera los tatuajes ofrecían la defensa mágica contra las mordeduras y picaduras de estas criaturas. Ellos traían también la buena fortuna en el matrimonio, la vida y la siguiente vida.

Utilice por favor estas imágenes libremente para sus propios requisitos y como una fuente de la inspiración. Sin embargo, para la propaganda, el uso promocional o profesional, contacte por favor al editor para el permiso y honorarios: info@hvd-publishing.com.

# Disegni Originari dell'India

I bei disegni contenuti in questo libro sono soprattutto raffigurazioni geometriche di animali, fiori, oggetti e divinità e sono ricamati su vesti, dipinti su muri e ceramiche, tracciati sui pavimenti come talismani ed anche usati come disegni per tatuaggi normali e all'hennè. Riflettono la vitalità, la cultura e le credenze dei popoli Indiani.

I disegni sono fortemente legati all'Induismo e al Buddismo. Il Serpente (naga), per esempio, è un seguace del dio Indú Vishnu, il protettore della creazione e del Buddha. I Naga appaiono frequentemente come guardiani intorno alle porte dei reliquiari Indú e Buddisti. L'elefante, considerato in India fortunato e sacro, simbolizza la prosperità ed il dio Ganesh. Fiori di loto, pesci, pavoni, triangoli e svastiche sono, in entrambi le religioni, simbolo di felicità e protezione. La divinità del loto è chiamata Lakshmi o Lakshmi-Padma (Loto Bianco), ed è la dea della prosperità e fortuna, potere e bellezza. Nel Buddismo un fiore aperto significa Illuminazione. Ne è anche importante il colore. Un fiore di loto rosa viene associato con il Grande Buddha; un fiore di loto bianco significa purezza. Nel Bengala, per esempio, per un Brahmino, un membro dell'alta casta ecclesiastica, era cosa comune rifiutare acqua da una ragazza che non aveva un fiore di loto tatuato sulla fronte.

Molti dei complessi disegni rappresentano simboli religiosi e sono tracciati come nodi infiniti. Nel Buddismo, un nodo infinito rappresenta la saggezza infinita del Buddha e l'unione tra compassione e saggezza. Nella tradizione e religione Tamil, tuttavia, questi simboli vengono disegnati sulle case e in prossimità di luoghi di culto. Questi simboli accolgono persone e Dei in casa, specialmente Lakshmi, la dea della prosperità. Vengono chiamati disegni Kolam e sono tracciati dalle donne ogni mattina sul pavimento fuori l'entrata delle loro case. Secondo la tradizione, le linee devono essere completate per evitare che gli spiriti maligni ne occupino il motivo. I disegni Kolam sono solitamente tracciati con chicchi di riso, farina o gesso, ma anche con vernici odierne. I motivi possono essere molto complicati e variano in grandezza; durante i mesi festivi, i templi vengono decorati con motivi che ricoprono migliaia di metri quadri. Motivi simmetrici creati con sabbia o farina colorata, sono chiamati rangoli. Non tanto tempo fa, le donne nel Tamil-Nadu di caste e tribú differenti si tatuavano questi motivi di labirinti sui loro corpi per assicurasi l'entrata in Paradiso, e una volta lí, per essere riconosciute dai loro antenati o mariti defunti. I tatuaggi servono soprattutto per migliorare l'aspetto femminile; sono i gioielli personali, ma funzionano anche come talismani. Un punto, per esempio, è un elemento comunemente usato contro l'occhio maligno, e raffigurazioni di scorpioni, serpenti, api o ragni offrono protezione magica contro i morsi e le punture di queste creature. Portano anche fortuna nel matrimonio, nella vita e nell'aldilà.

Le immagini contenute possono essere usate gratuitamente per scopi personali e come fonte d'ispirazione. Tuttavia, per utilizzo commerciale, promozionale o professionale, vi preghiamo di contattare l'editore per ricevere il permesso ed i diritti per l'utilizzo: info@hvd-publishing.com.

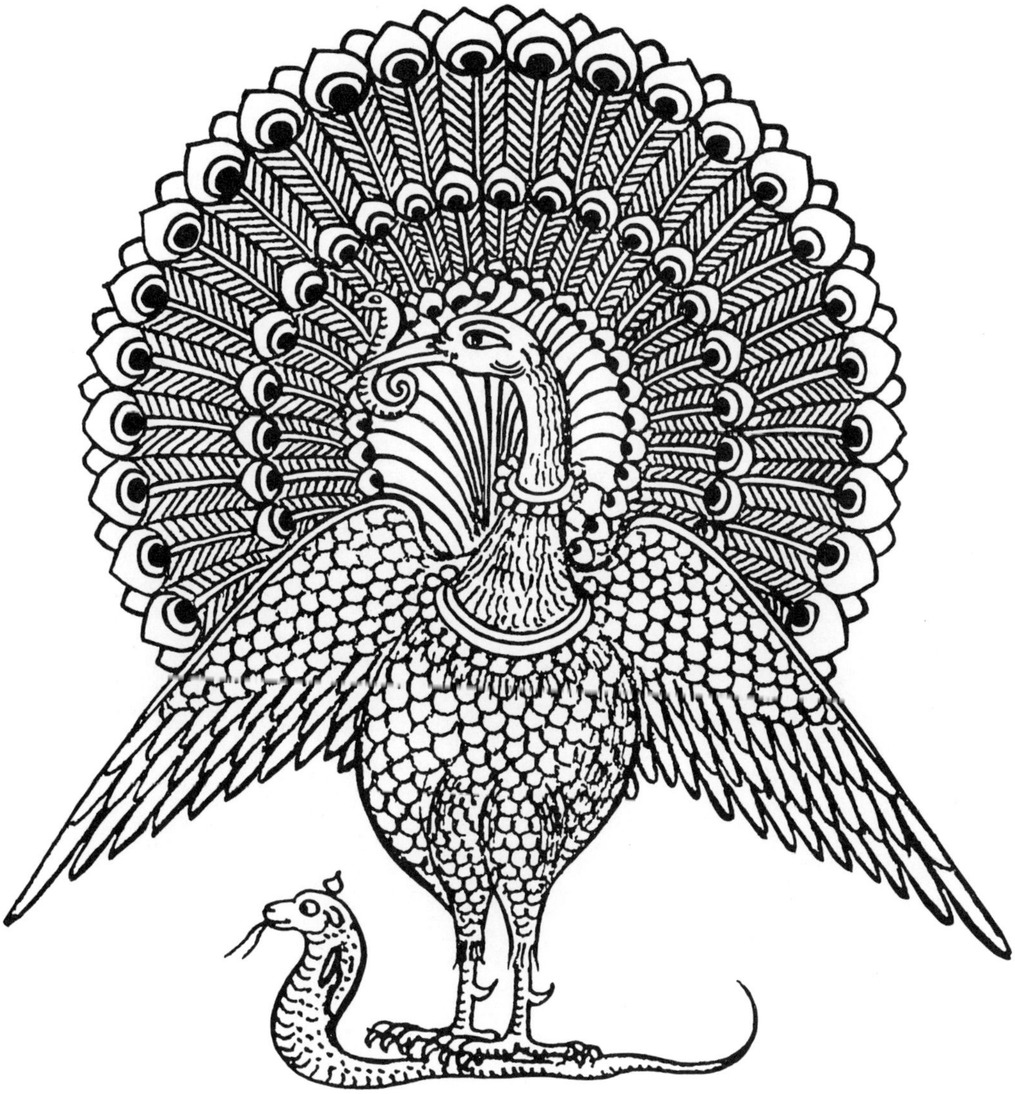

Peacock

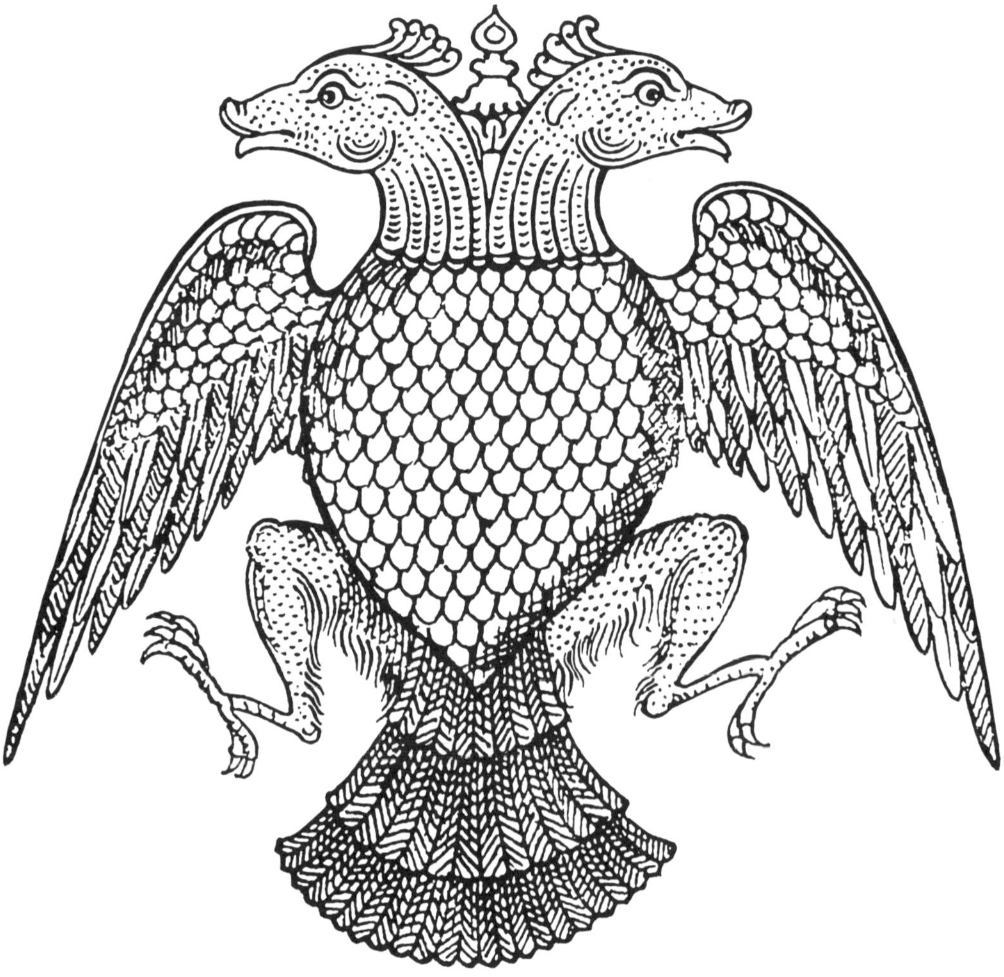

Bird with two heads

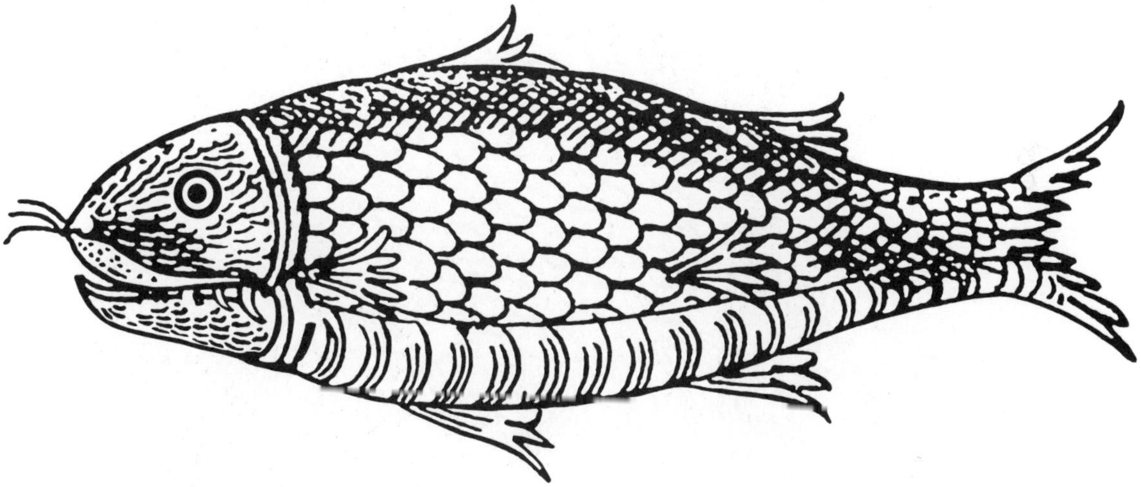



Fish

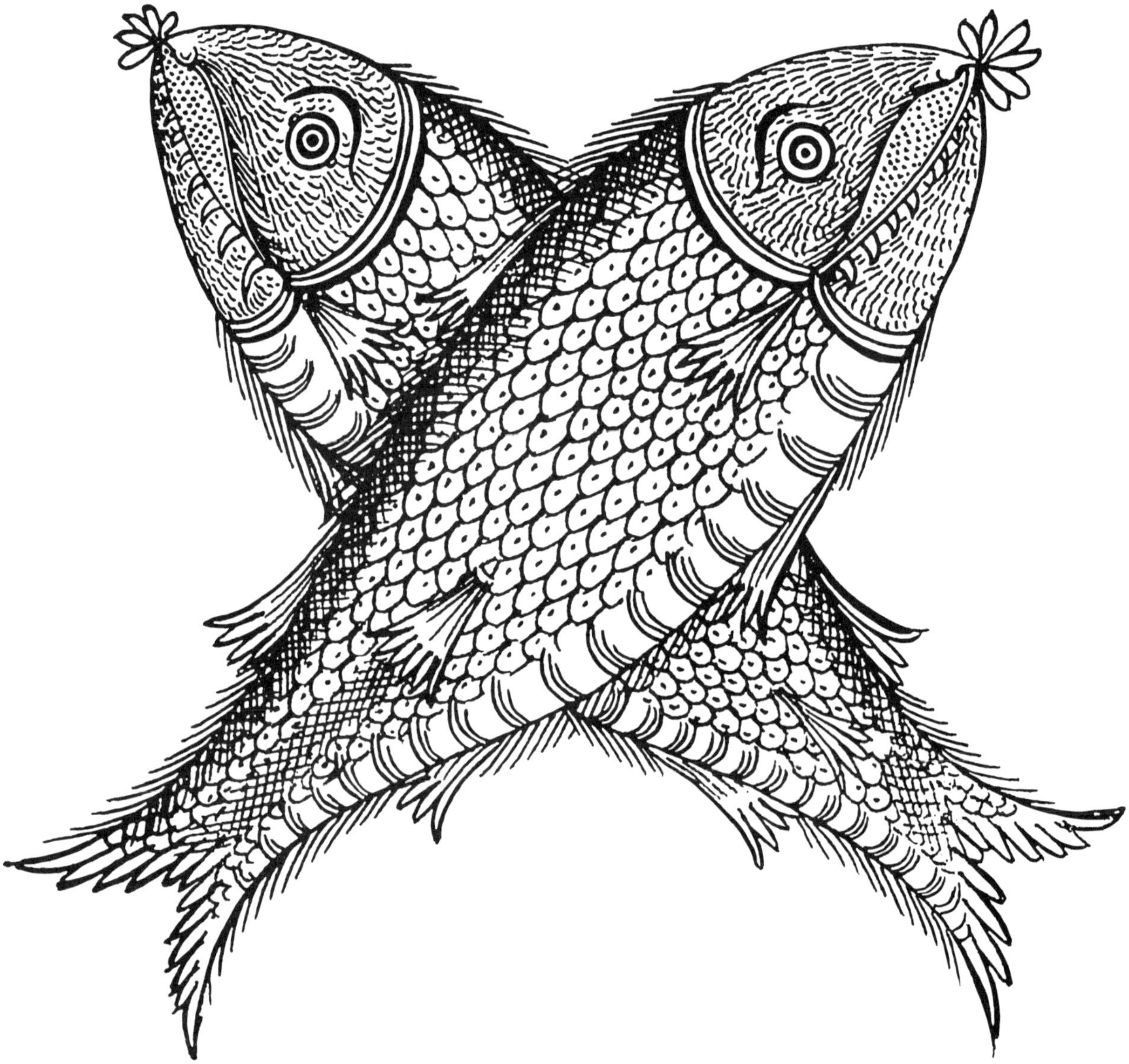

Pair of fish

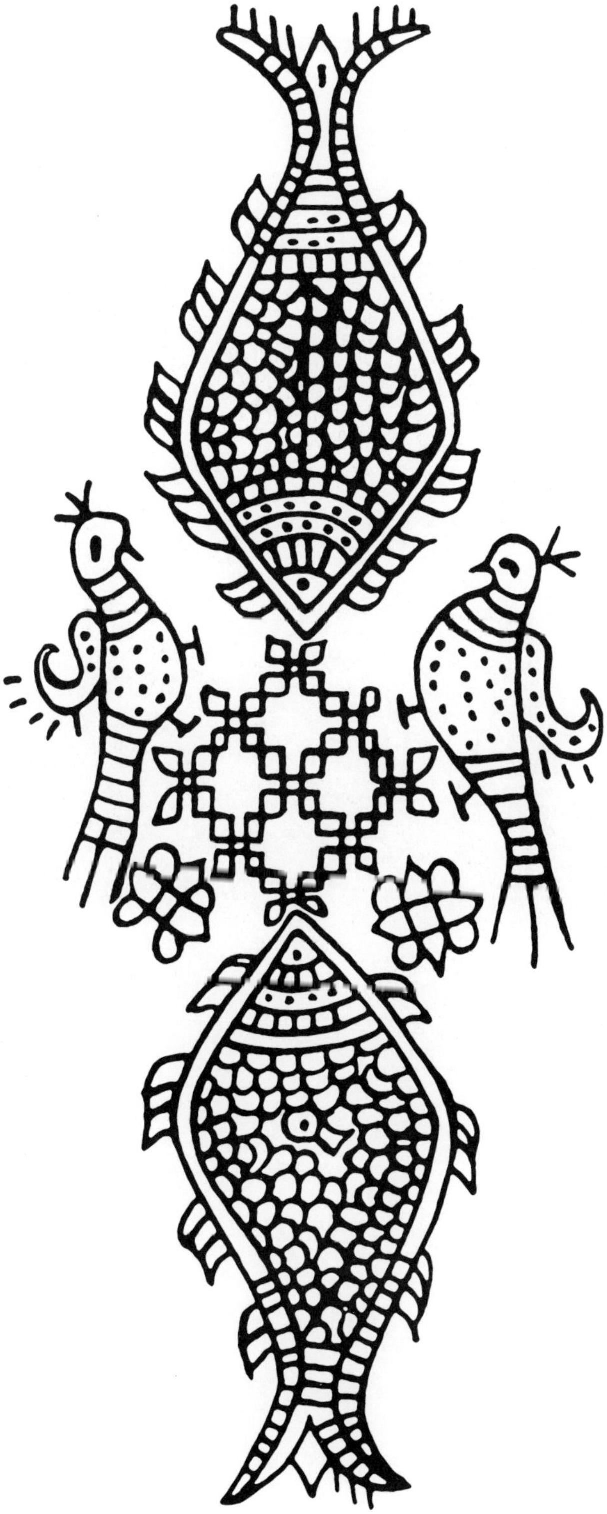

Parrot fish

16

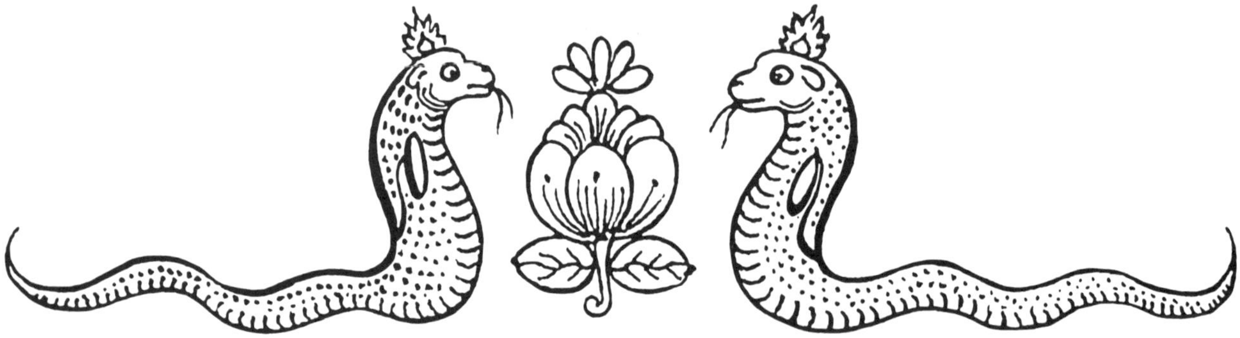

Two snakes

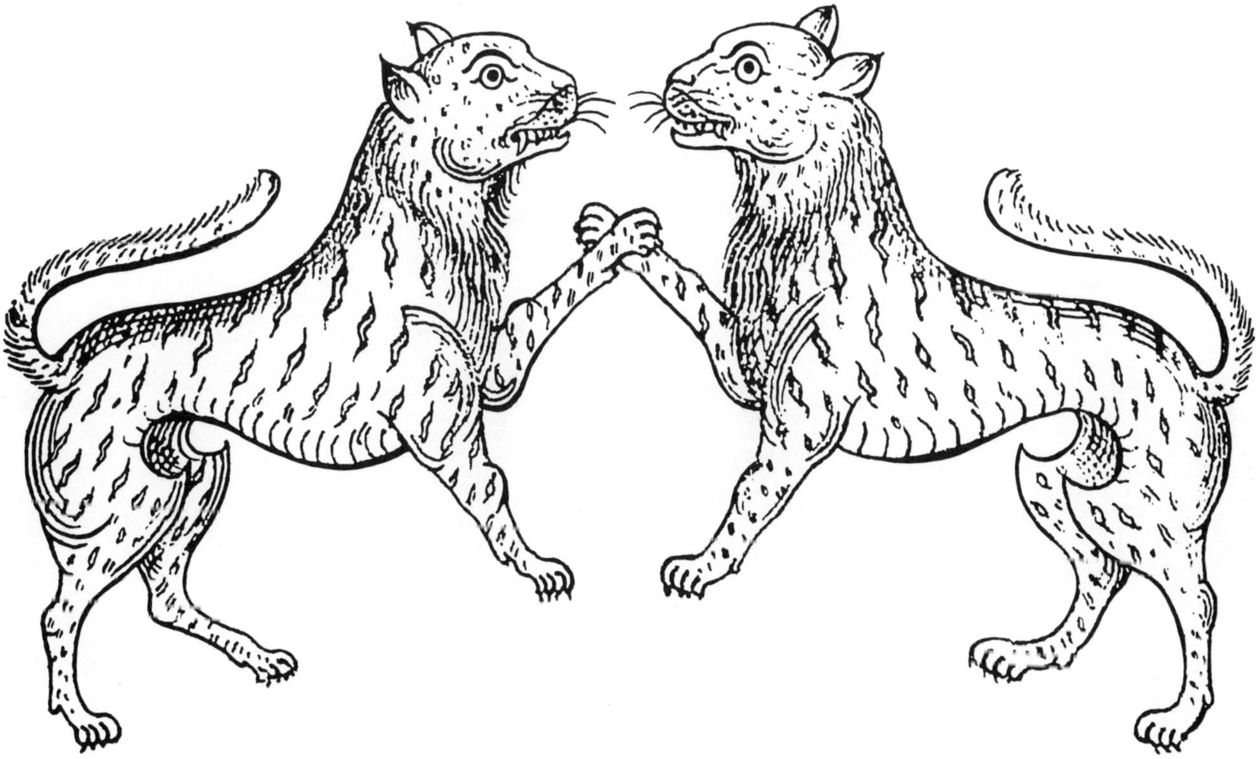



Pair of tigers

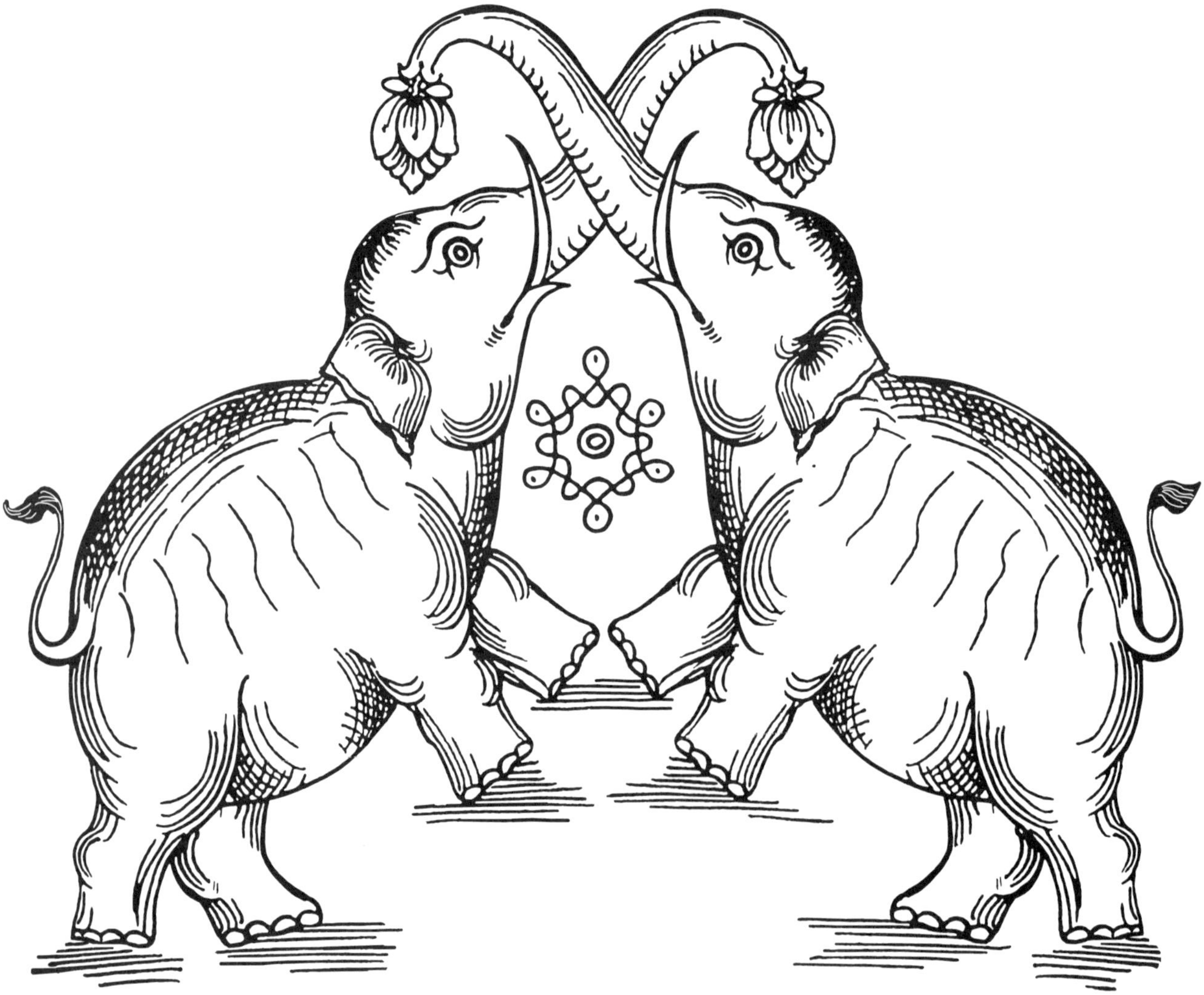

Intertwined elephants

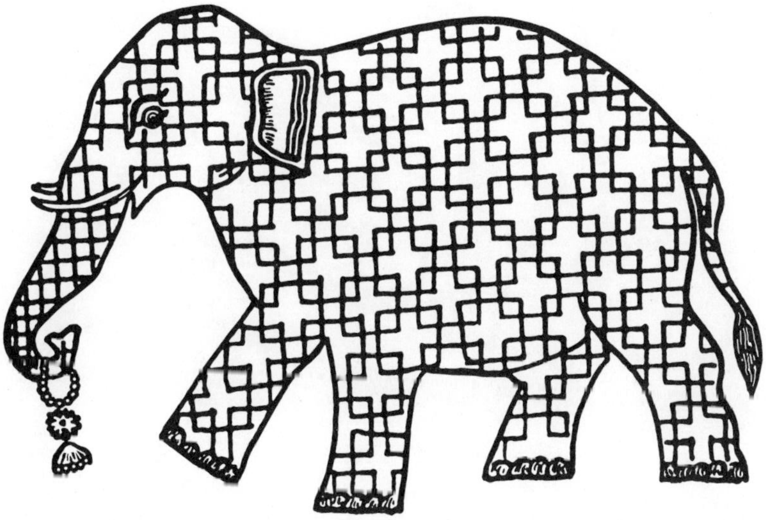



Elephant

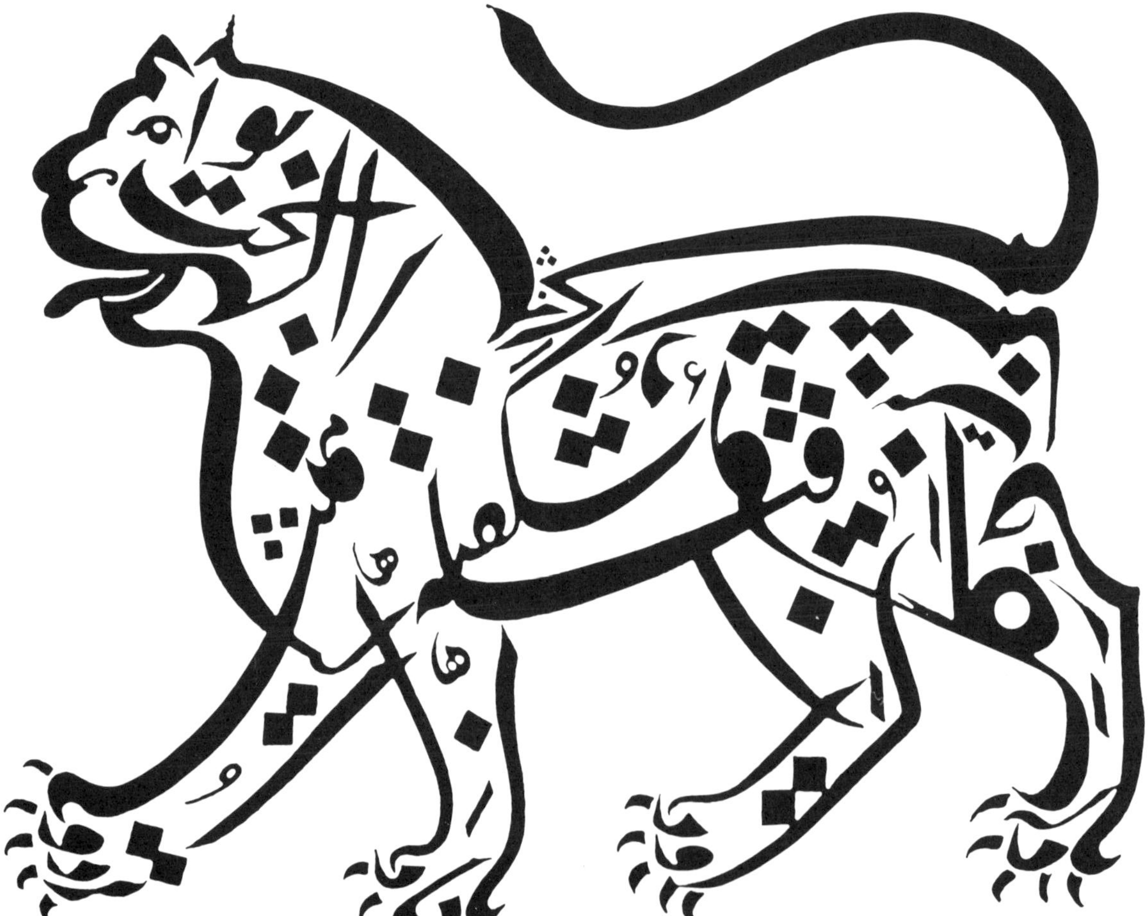

Tiger

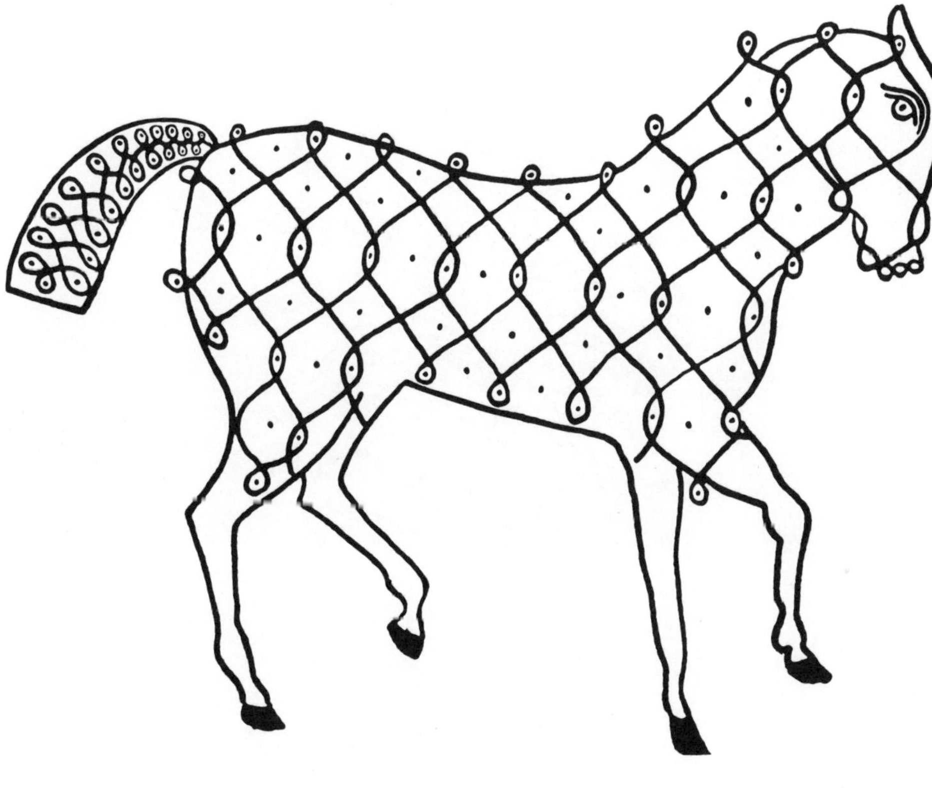



Horse

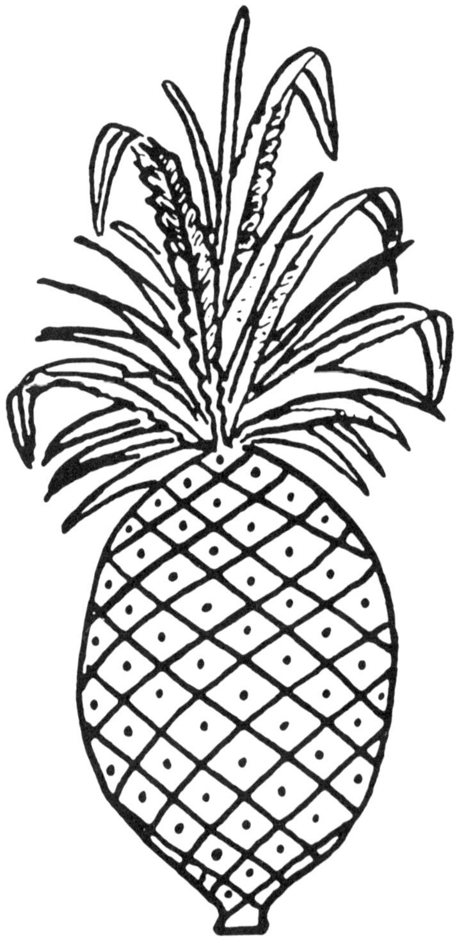

Pineapple

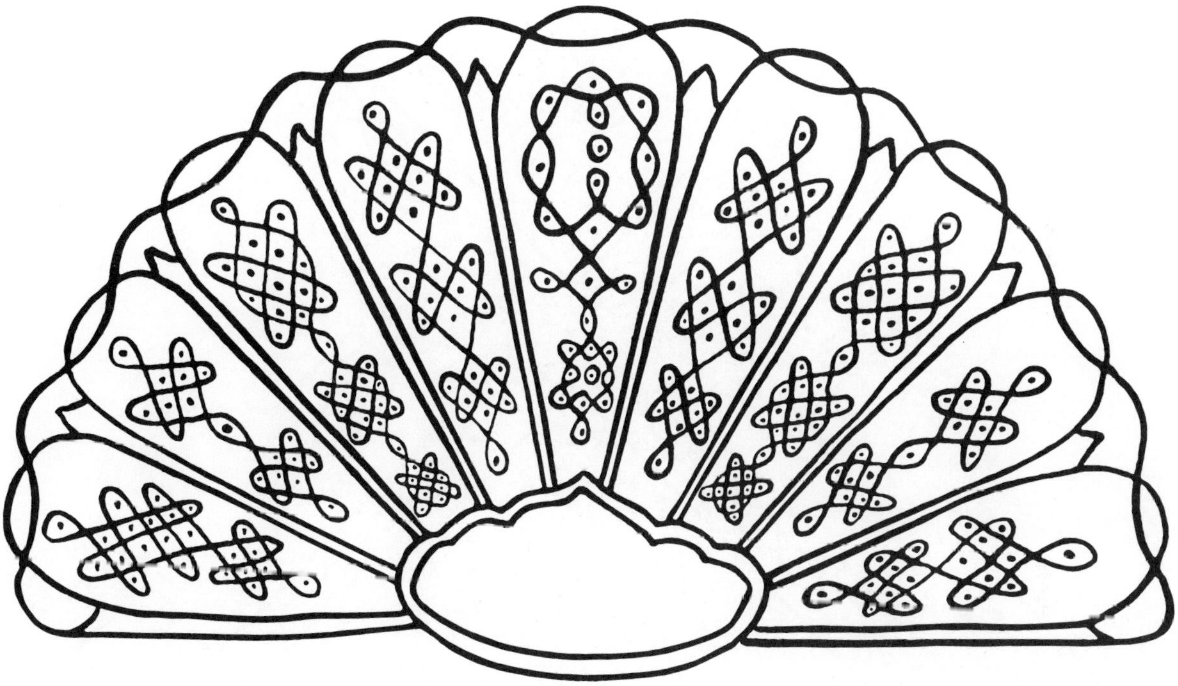



Rangoon fan

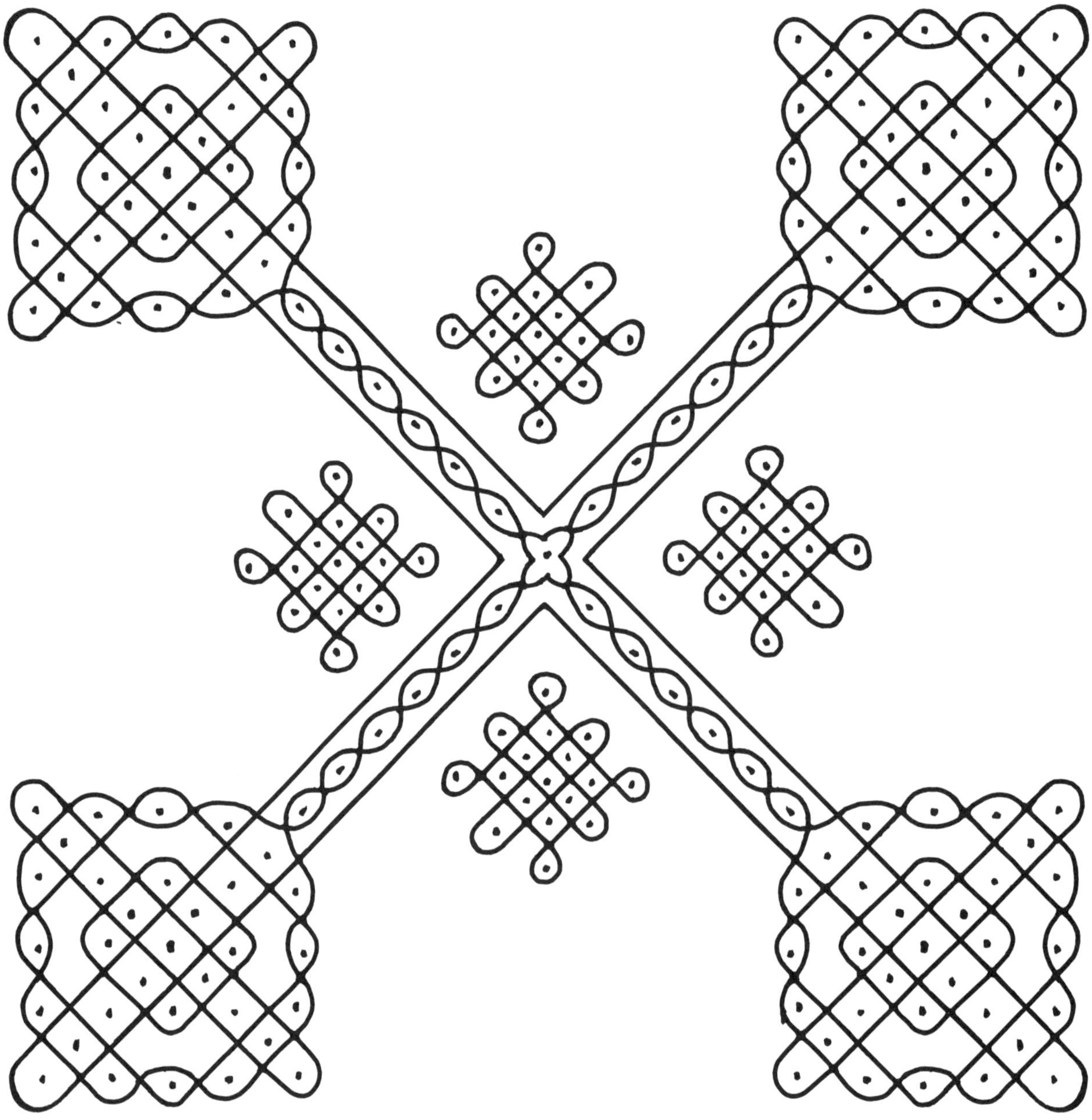

Kite

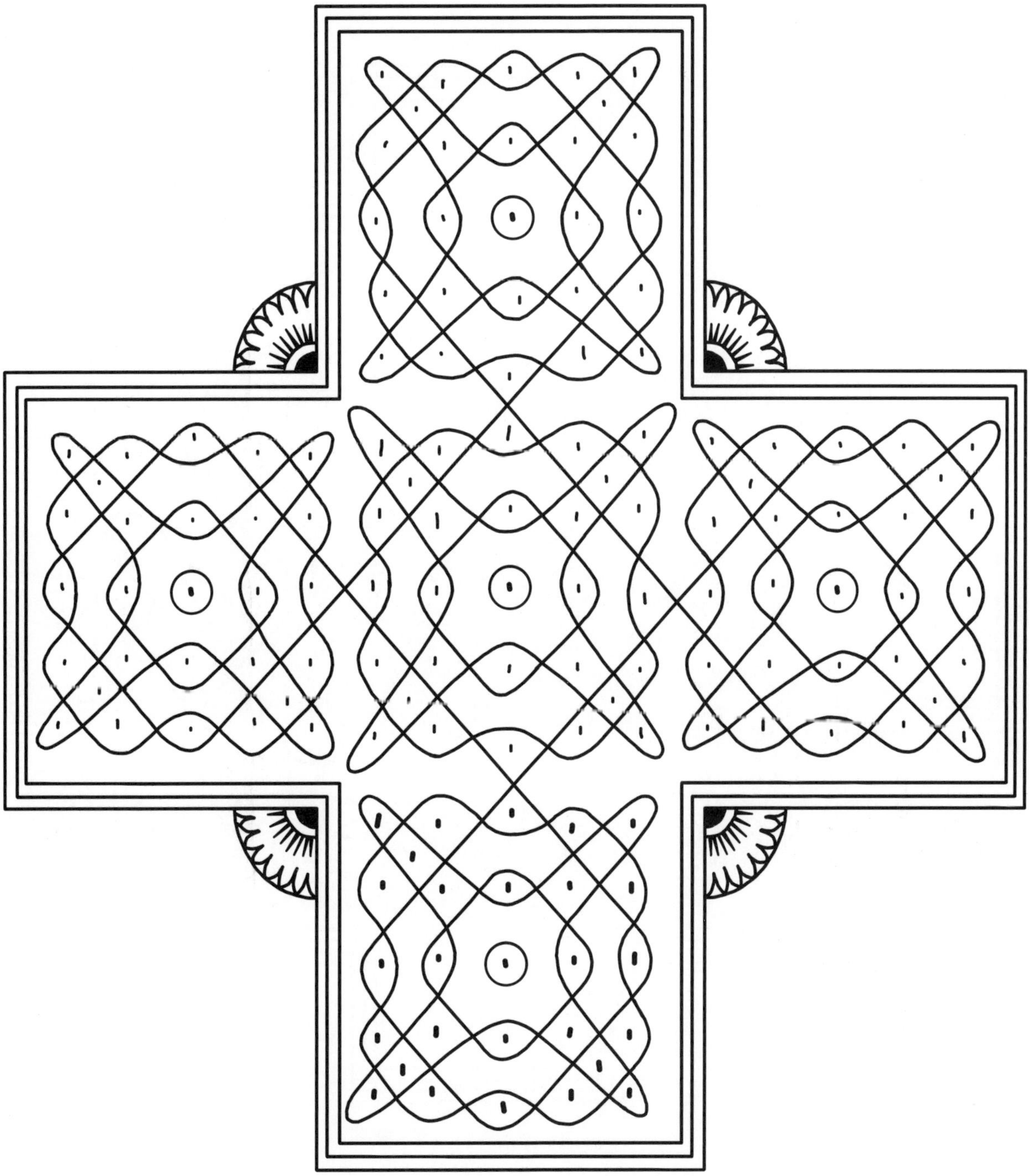

Sacrificial chamber

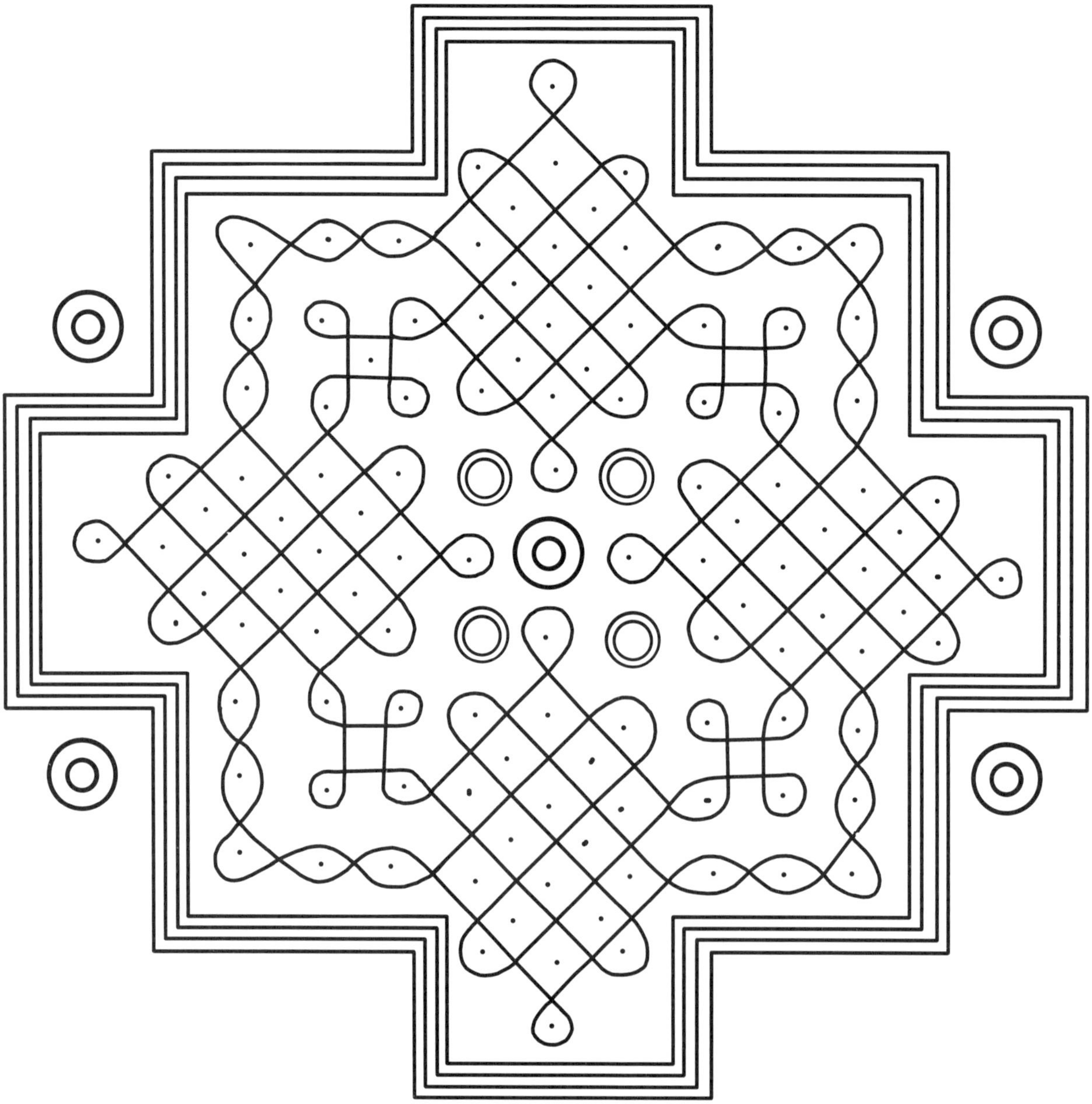



Pond with patterns

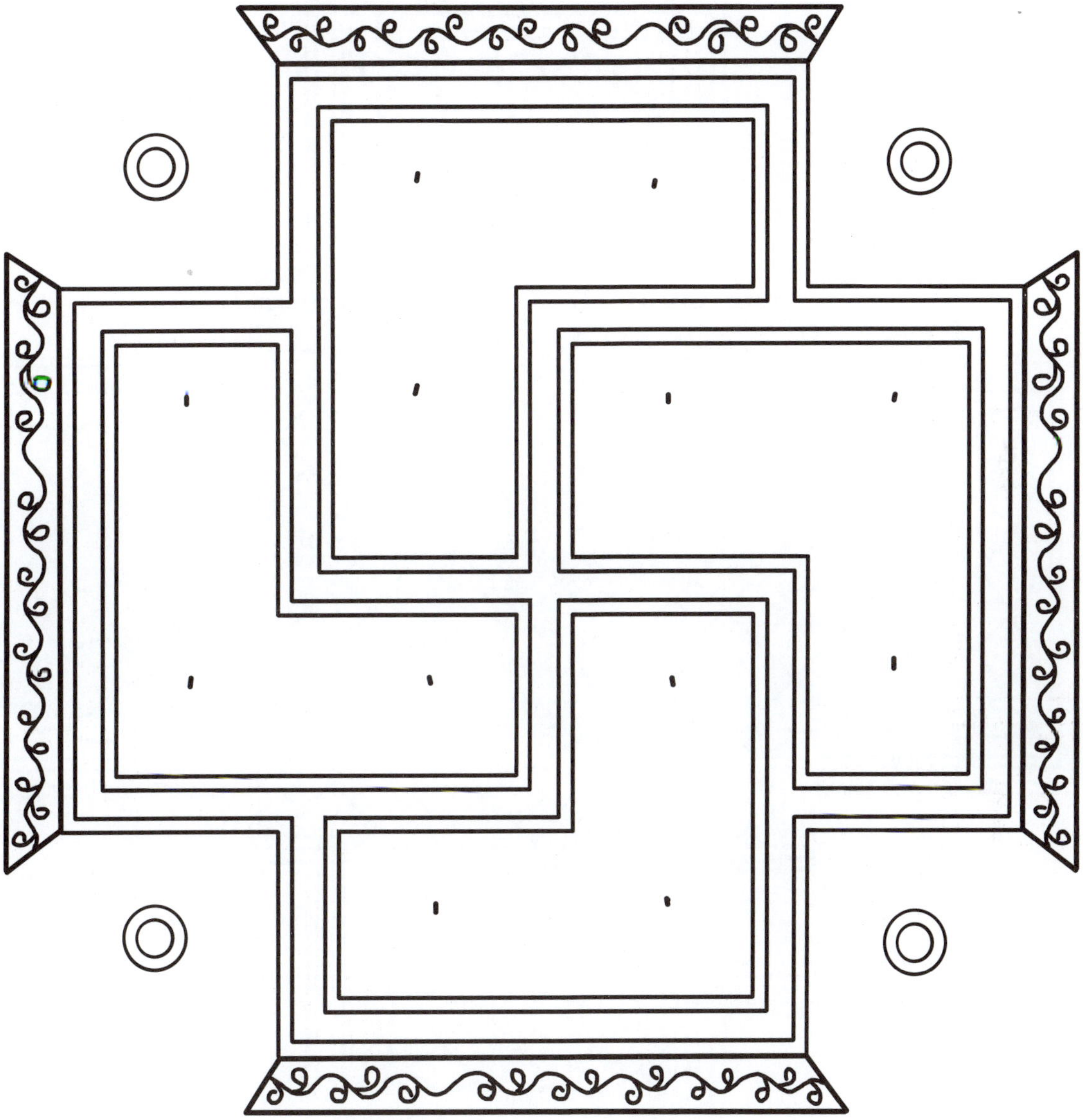



Sacrificial chamber

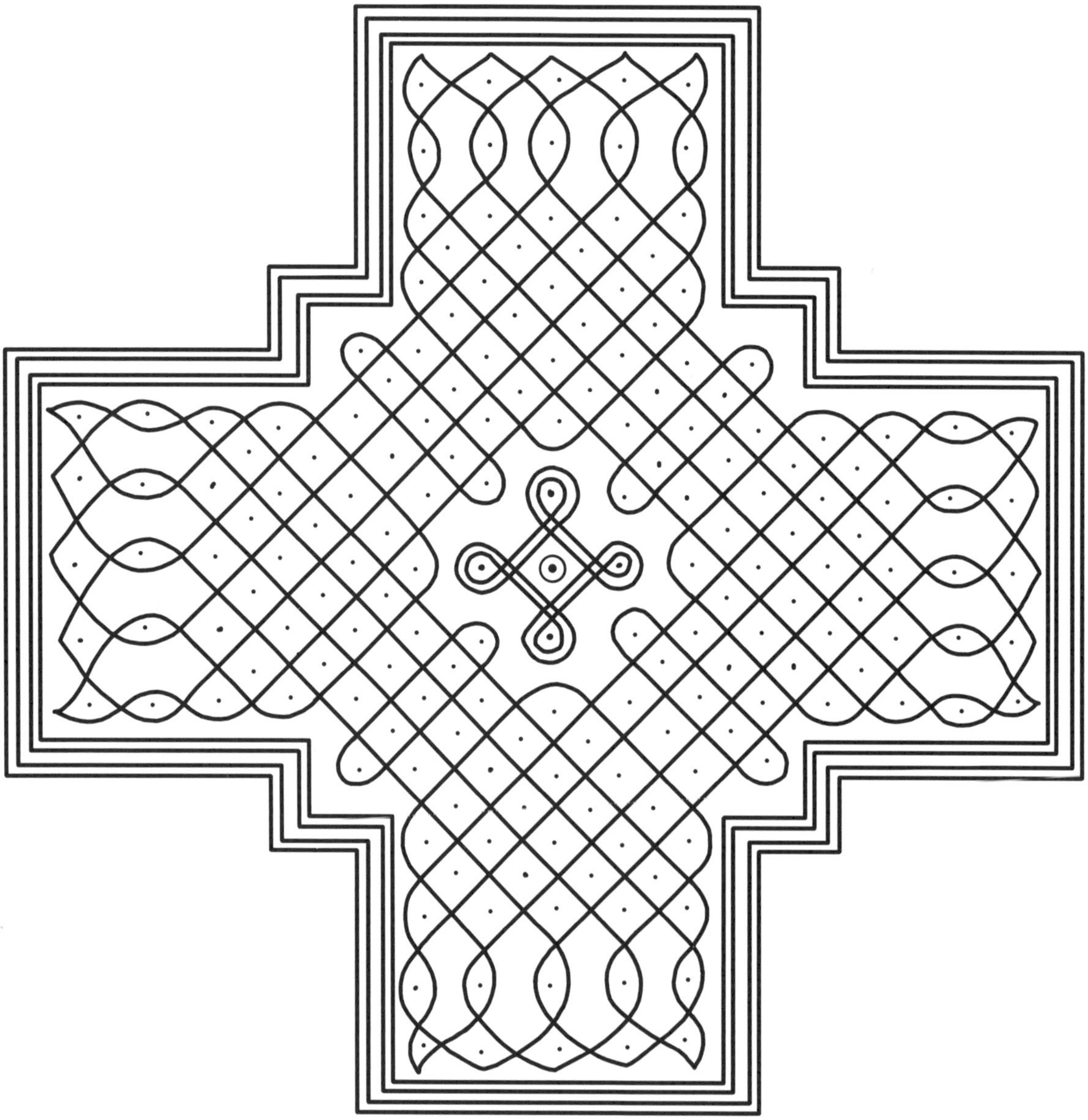

Altar for rituals

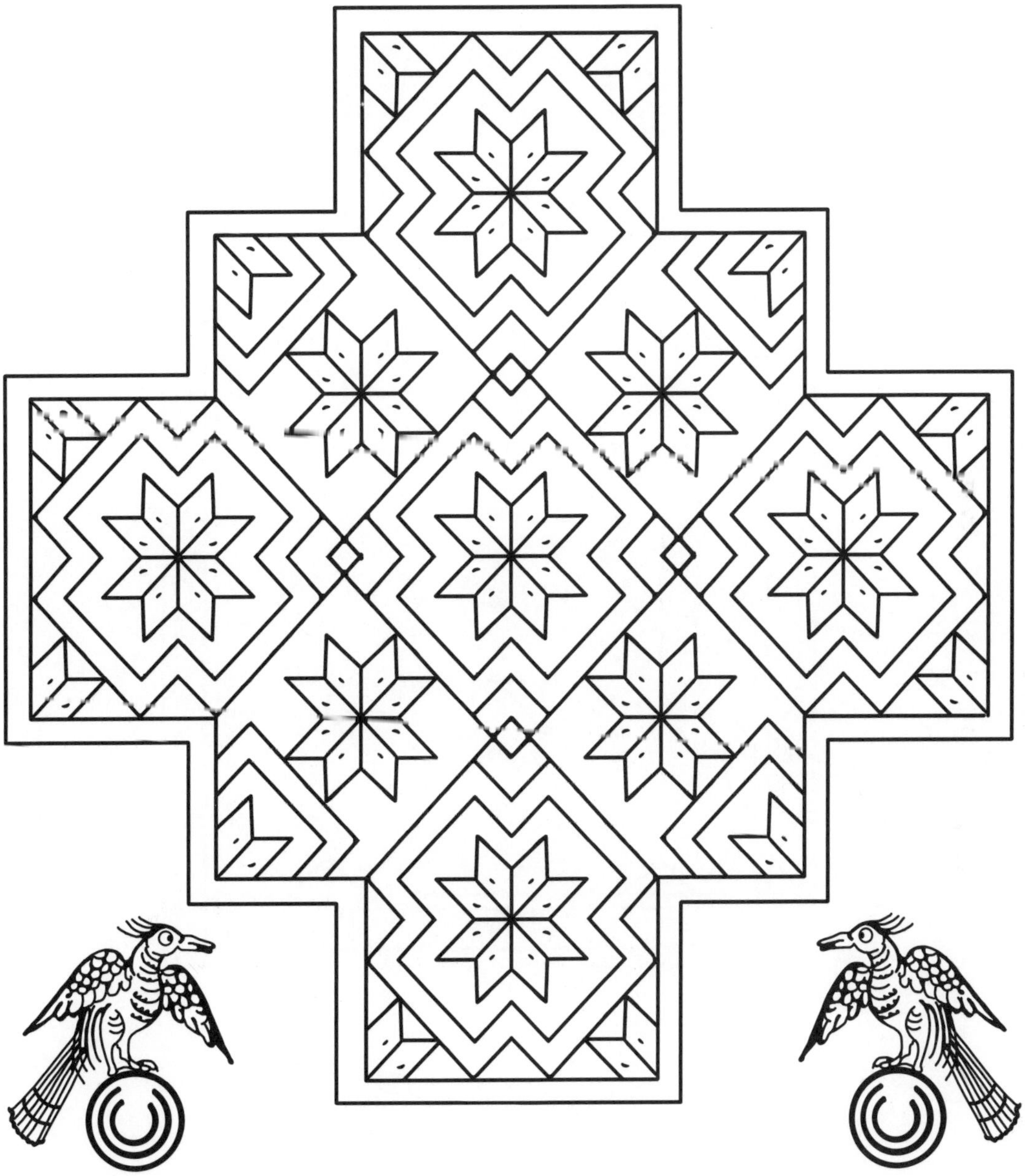



Wedding altar

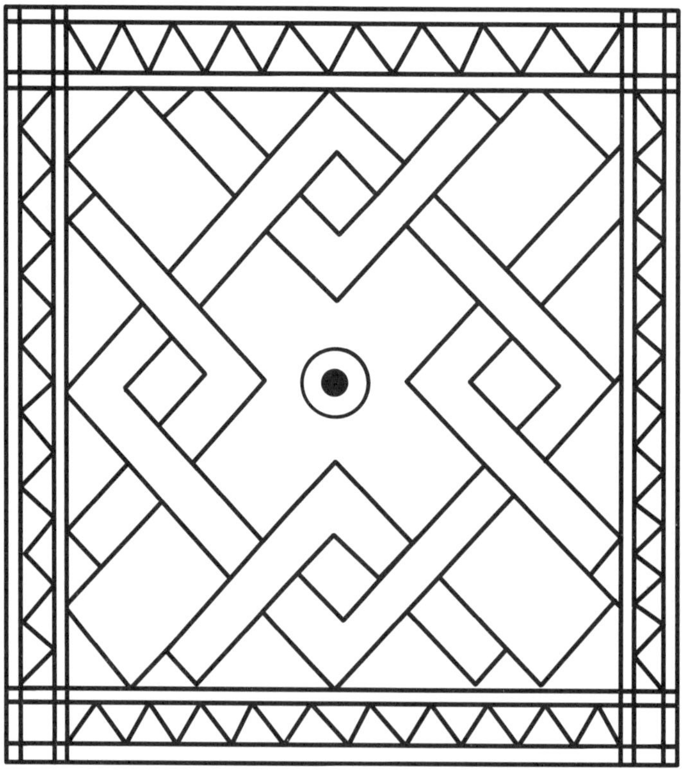



Knot

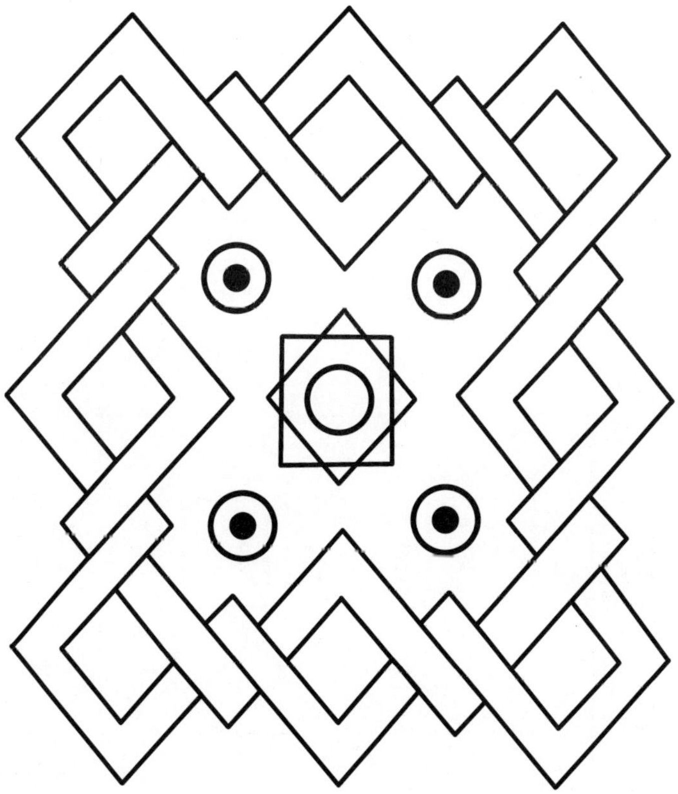

Knot

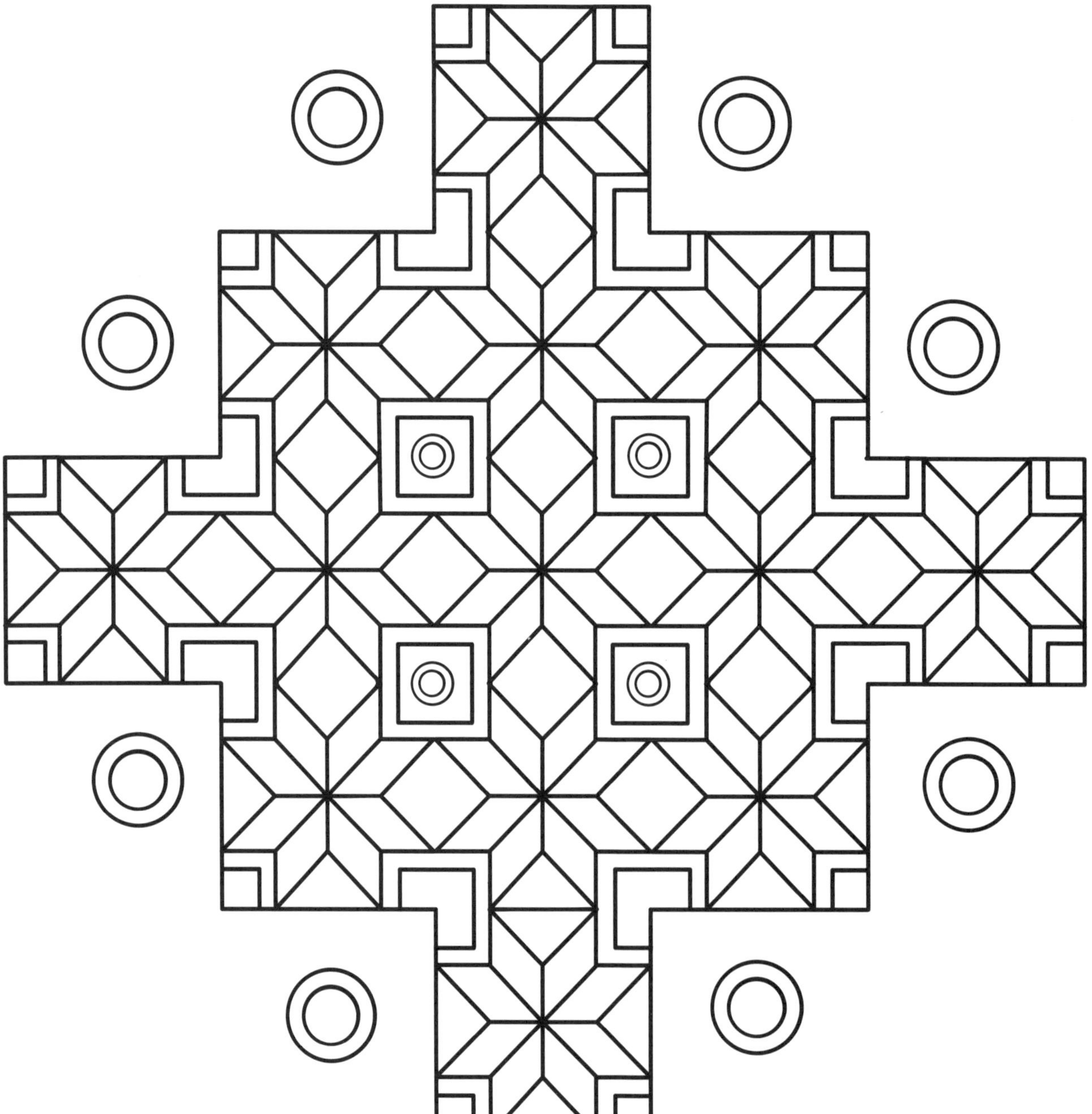

Ludo game

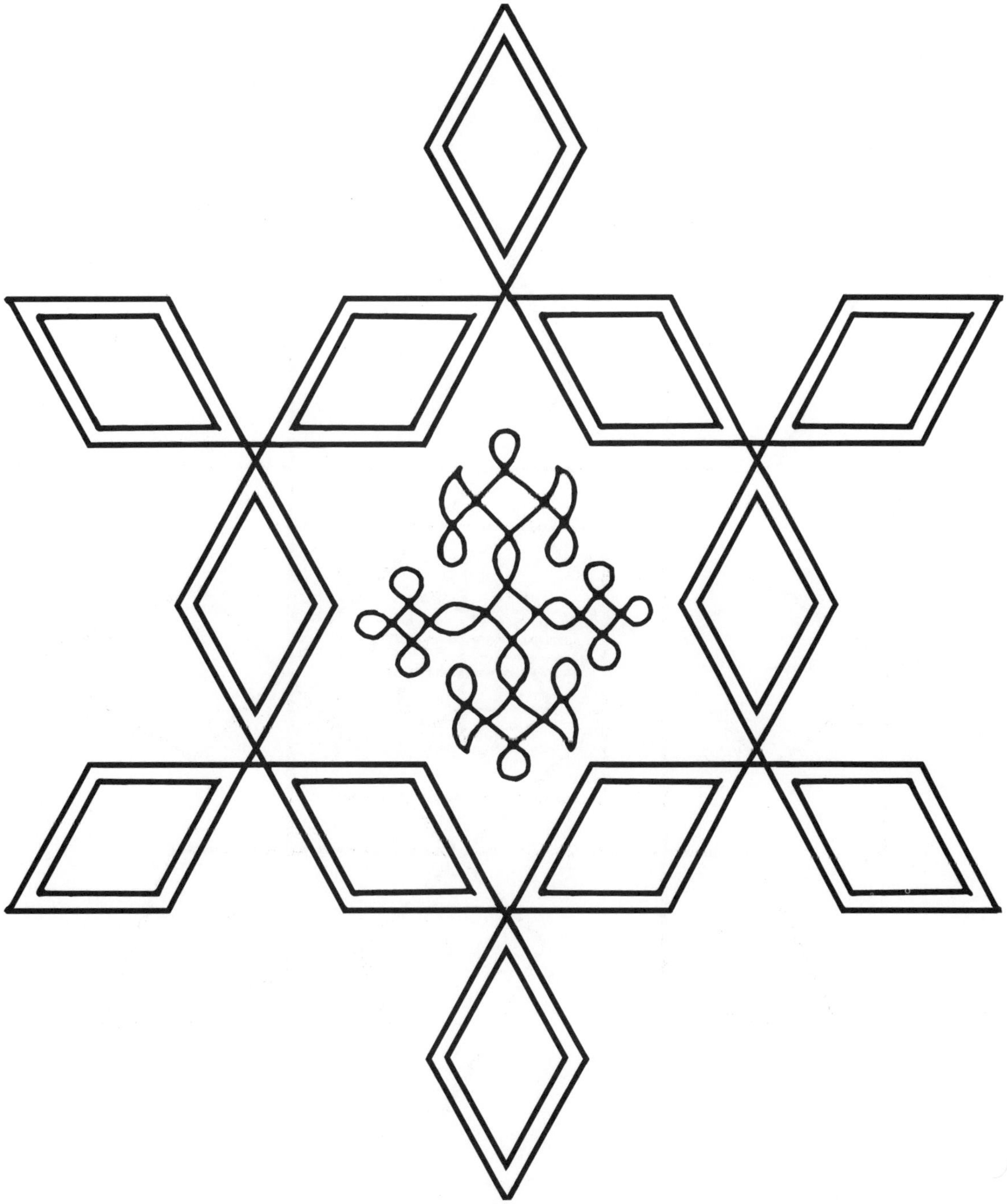



Lastar tray

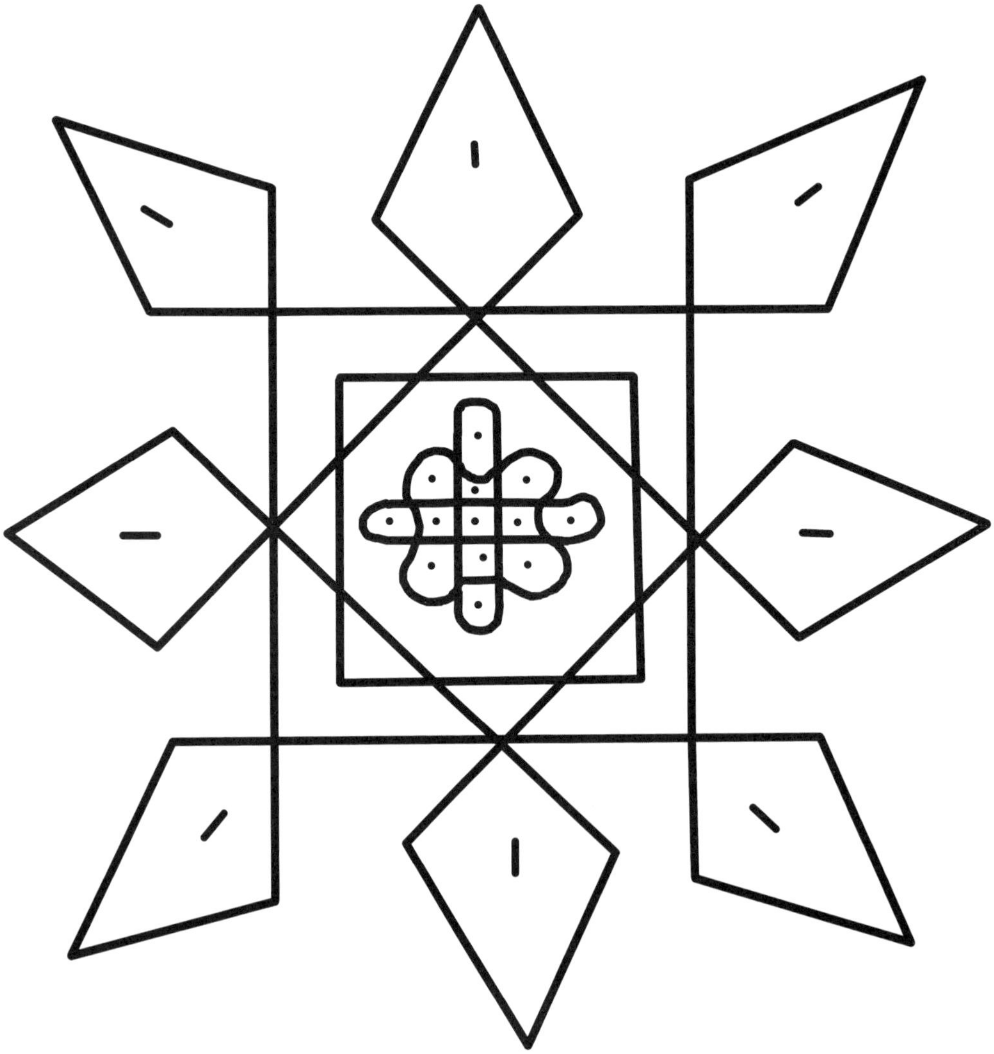



Lastar tray

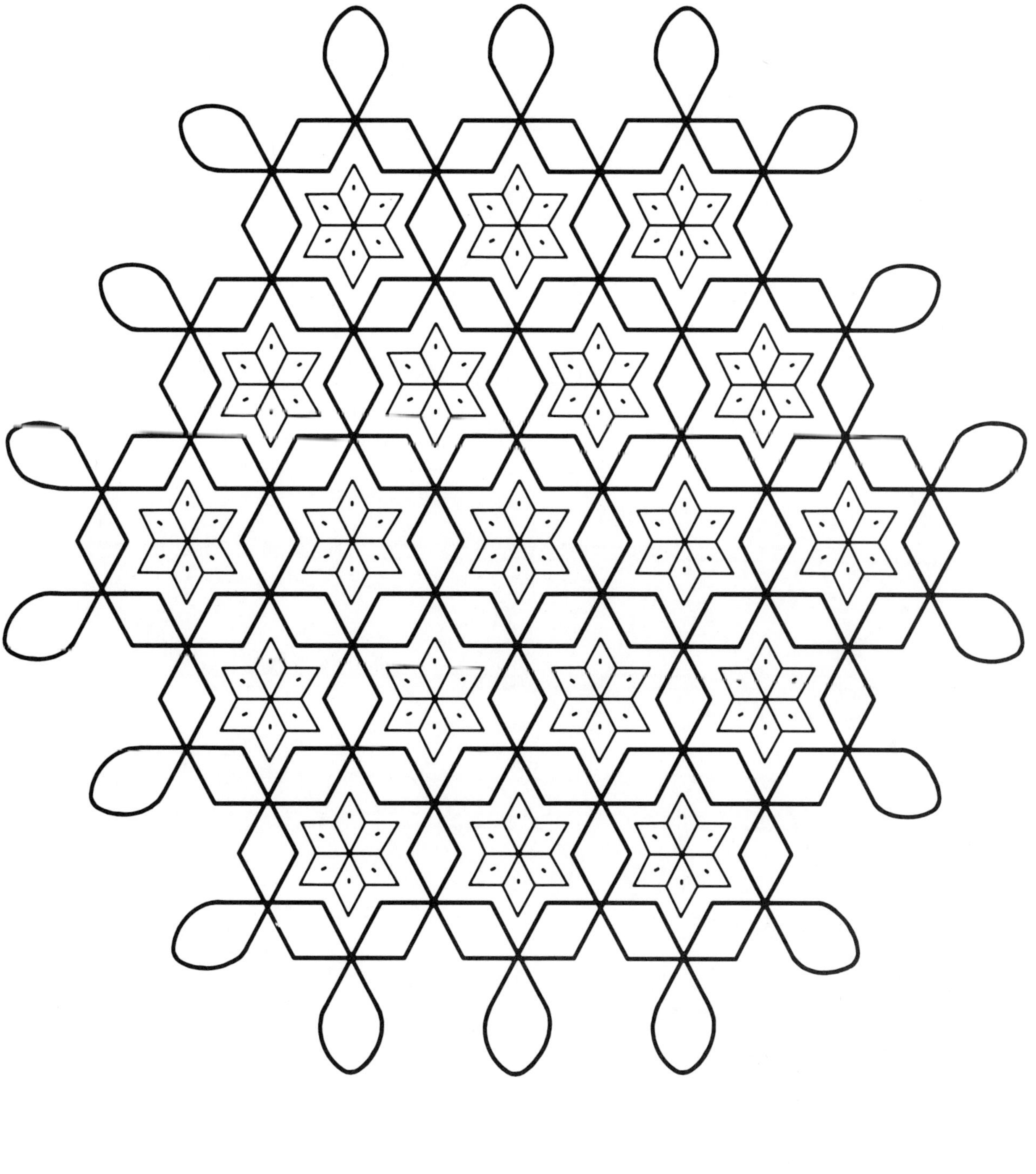

35

Vilvam-leaf

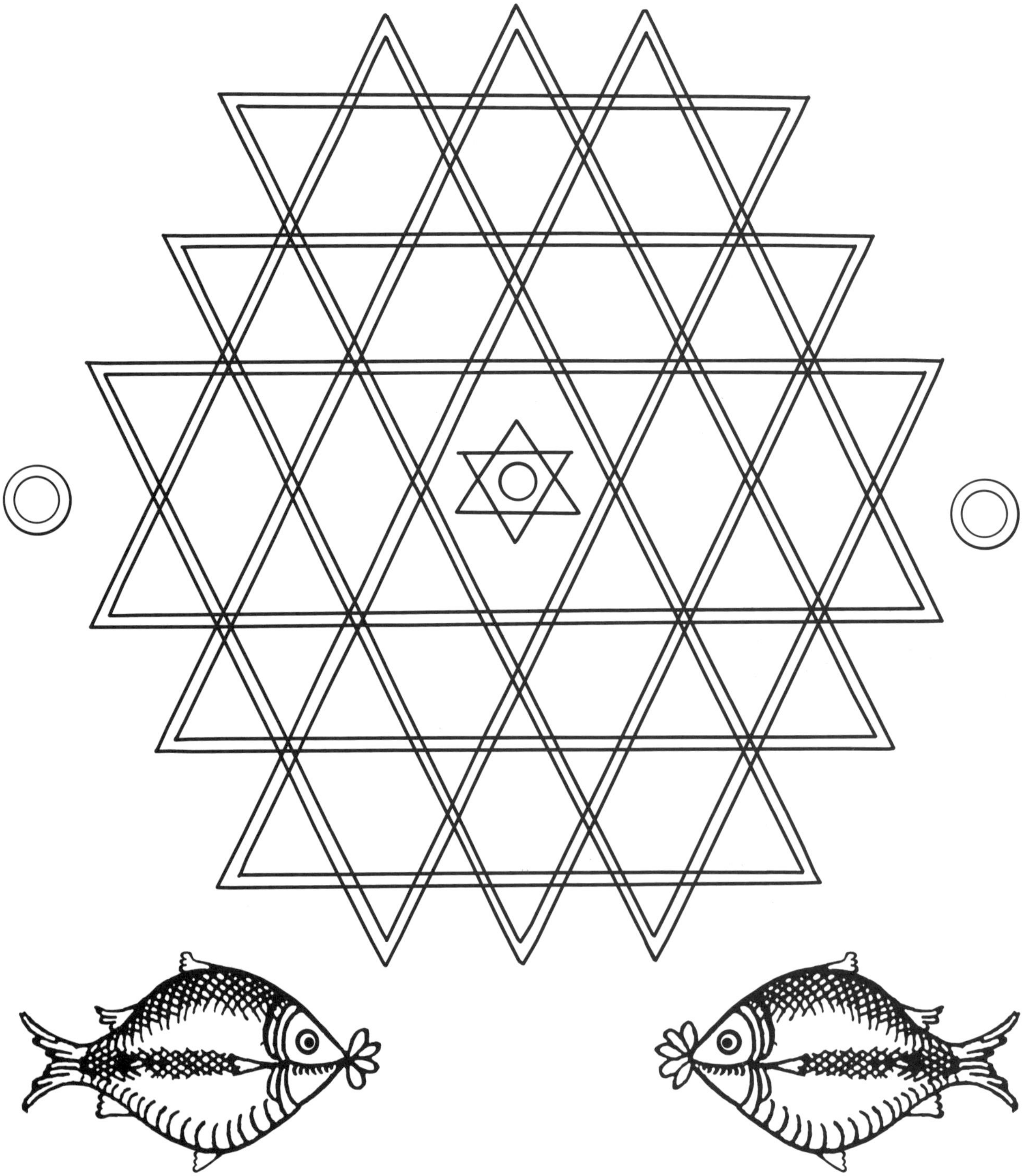



Chakra for sacrifice

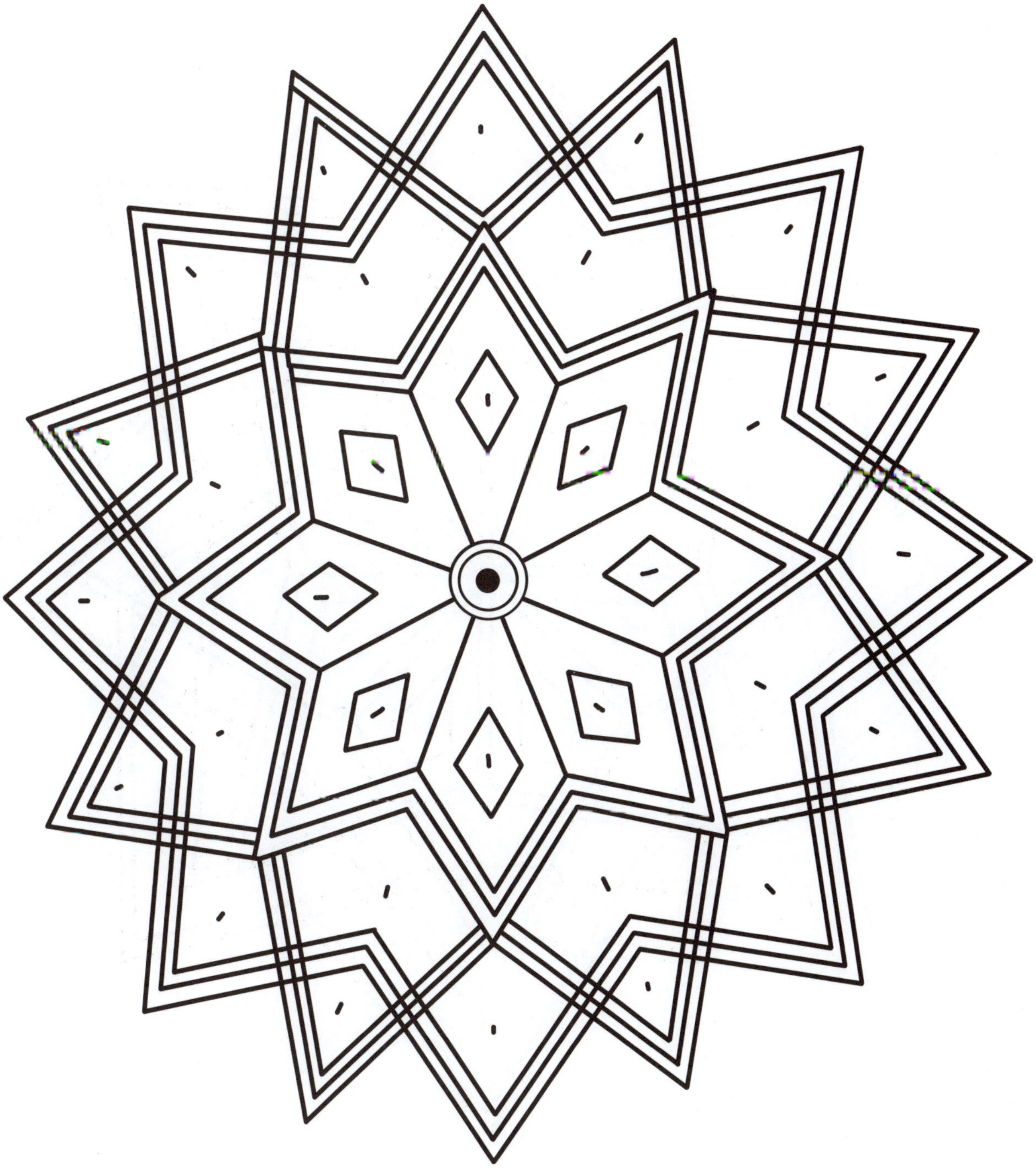

Angled lotus

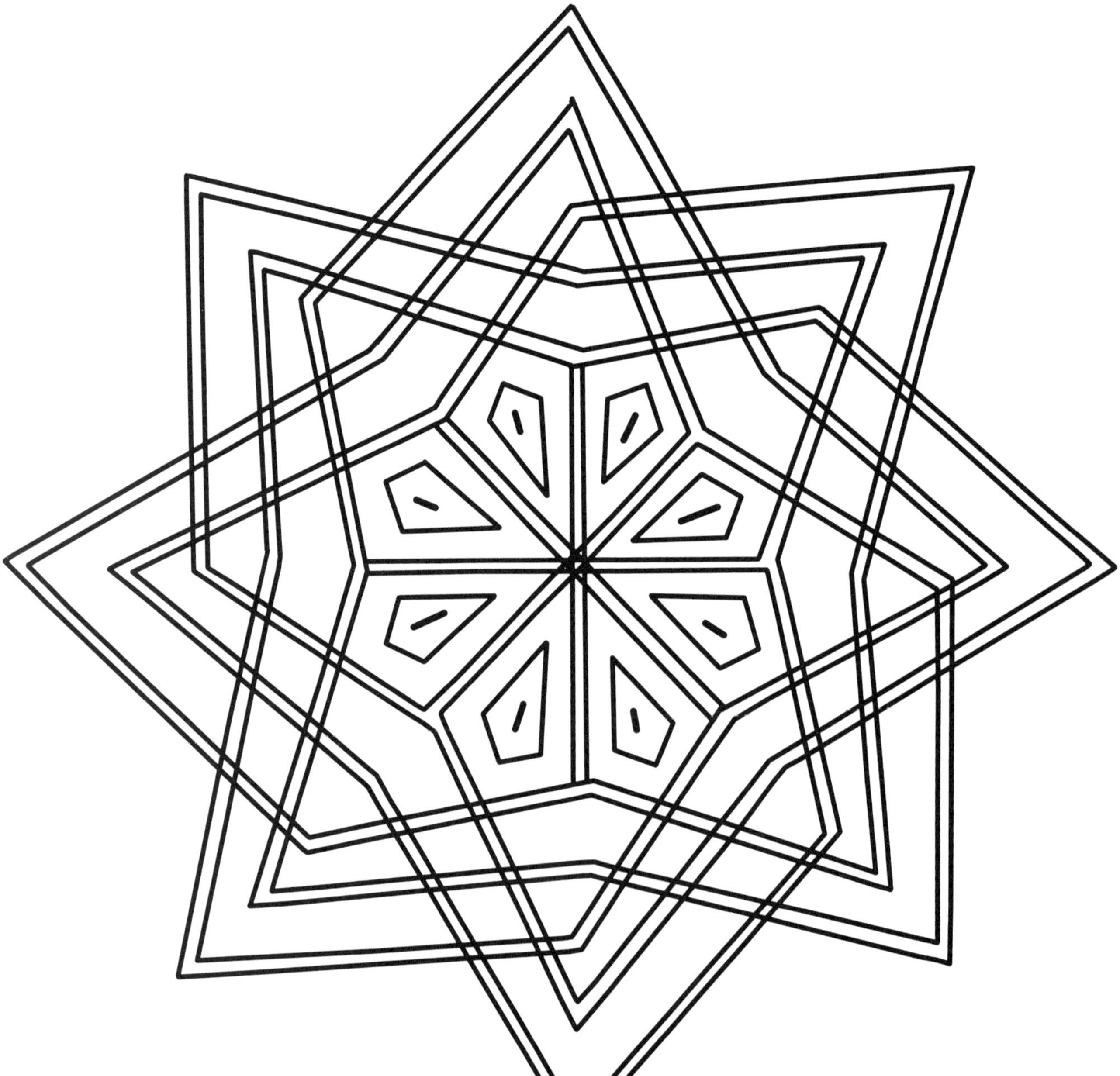

Angled chakra

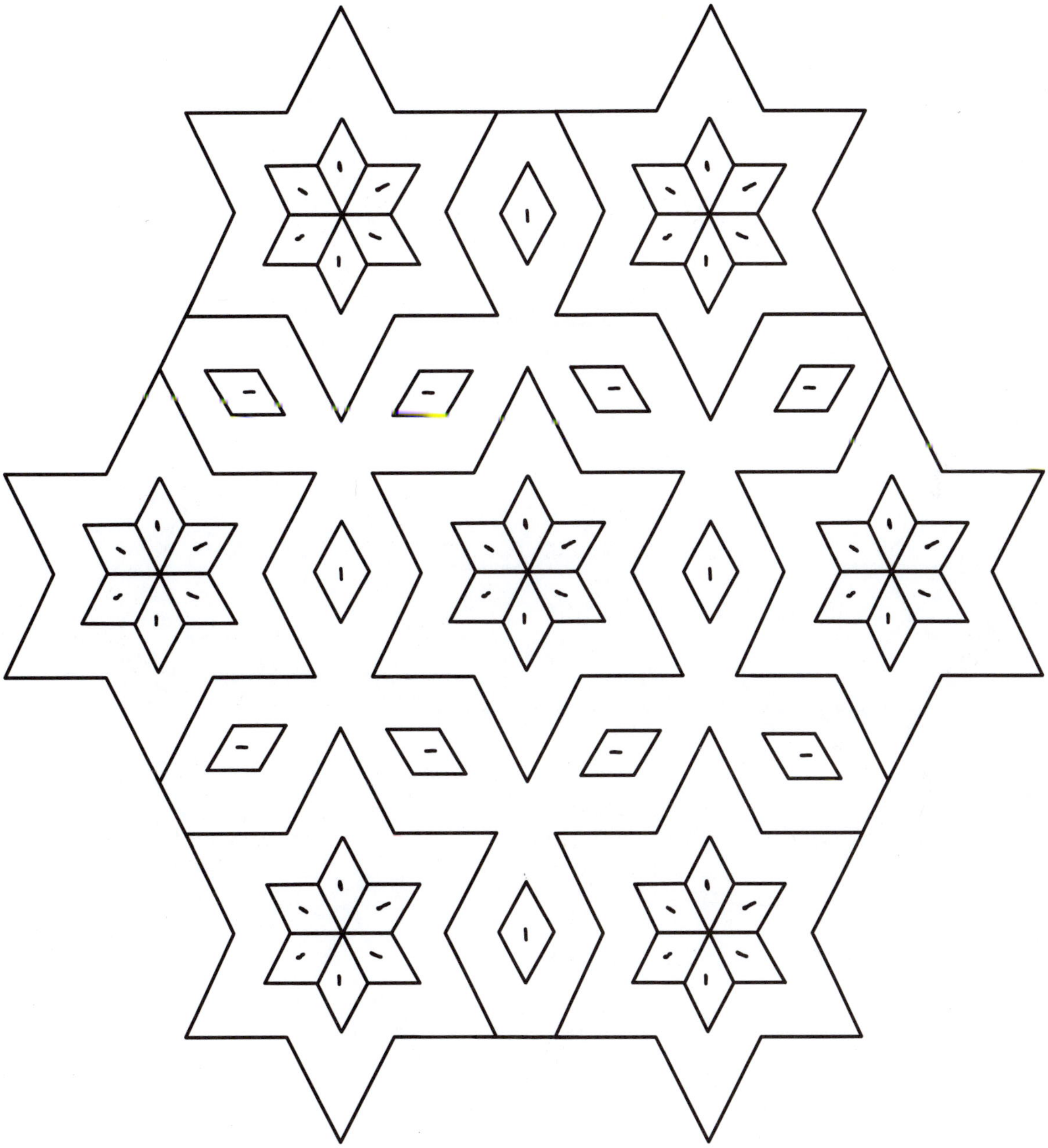

Vilvam leaf

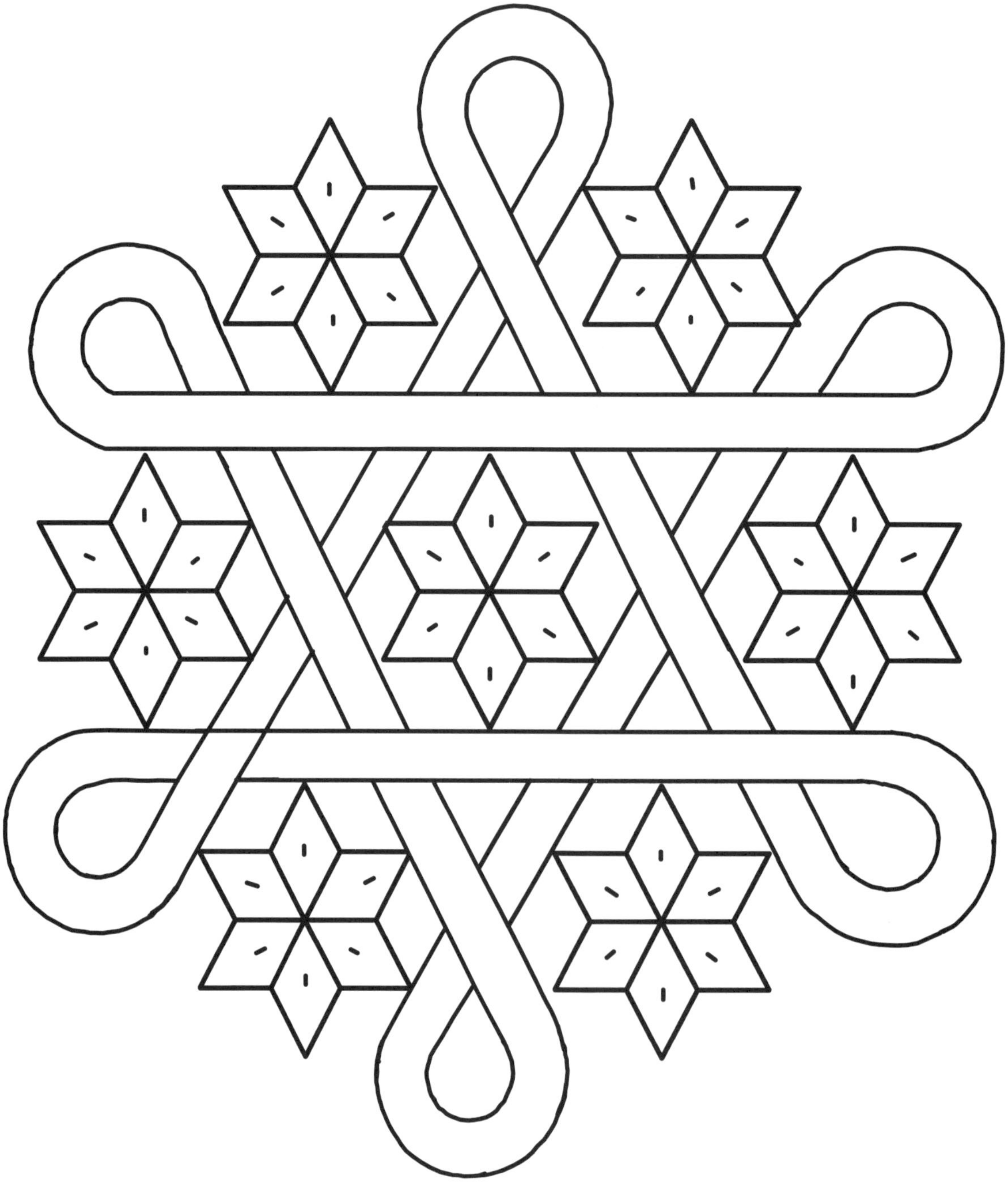



Tuttippu flower

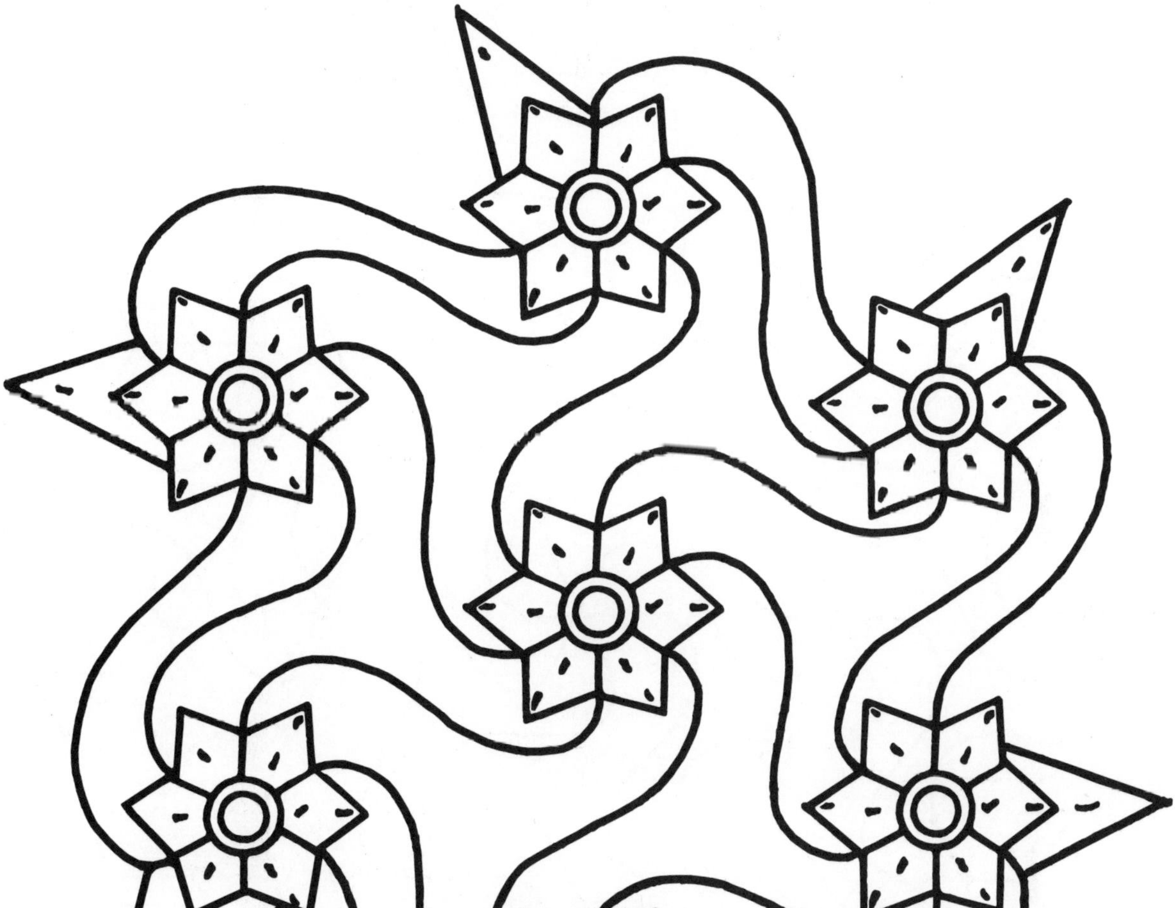

Talisman

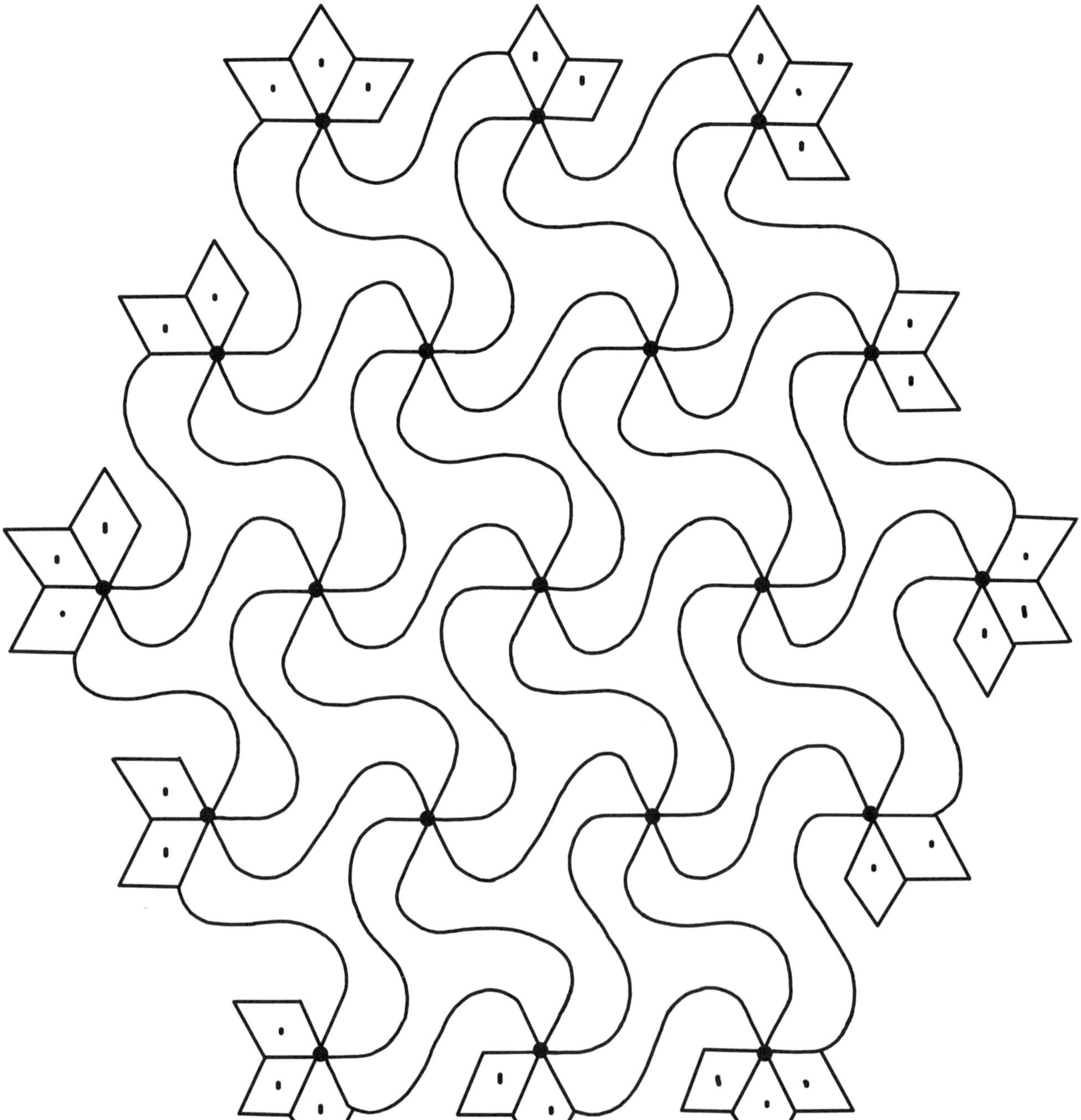



Nelli fruit

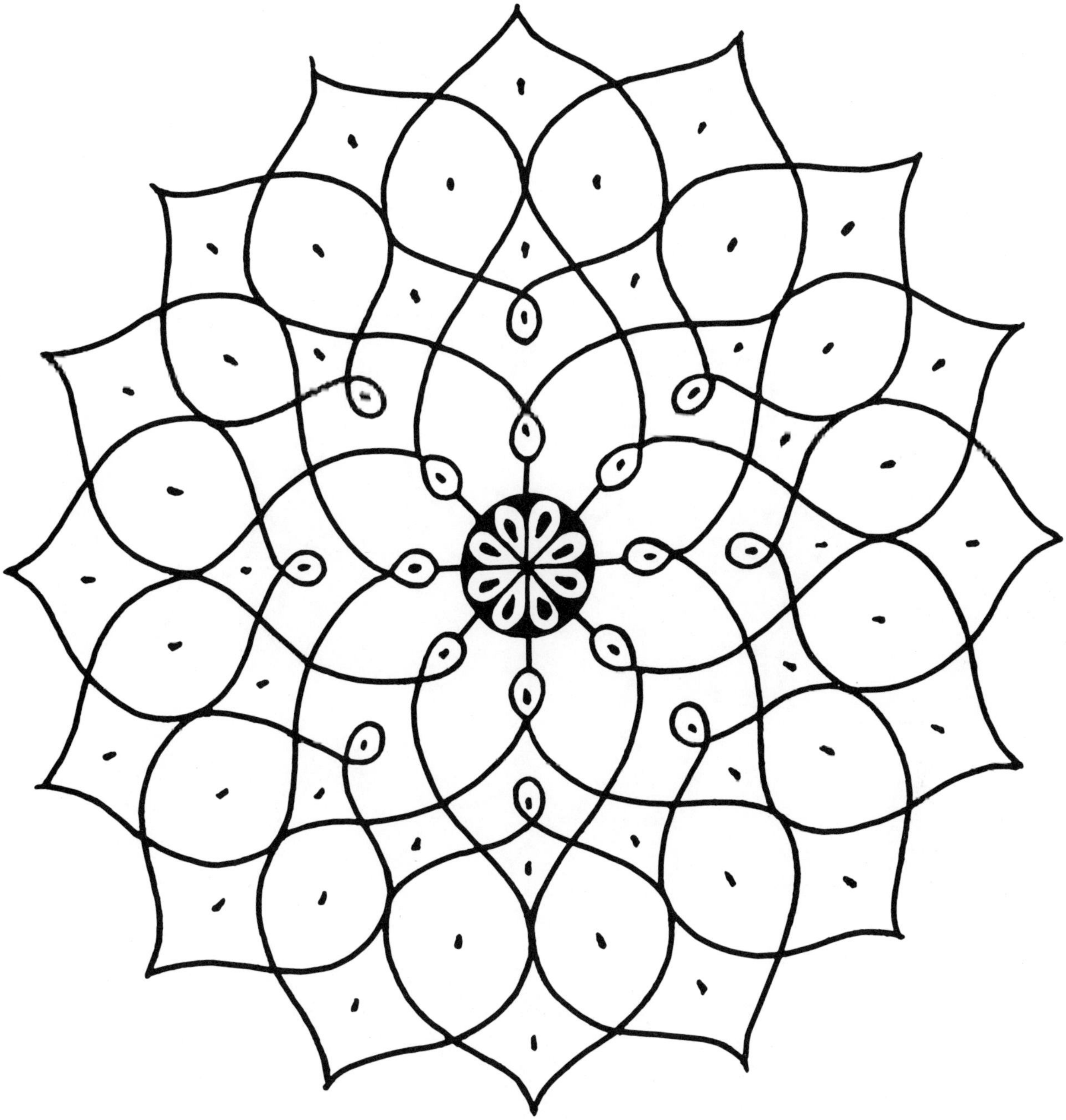

Lotus

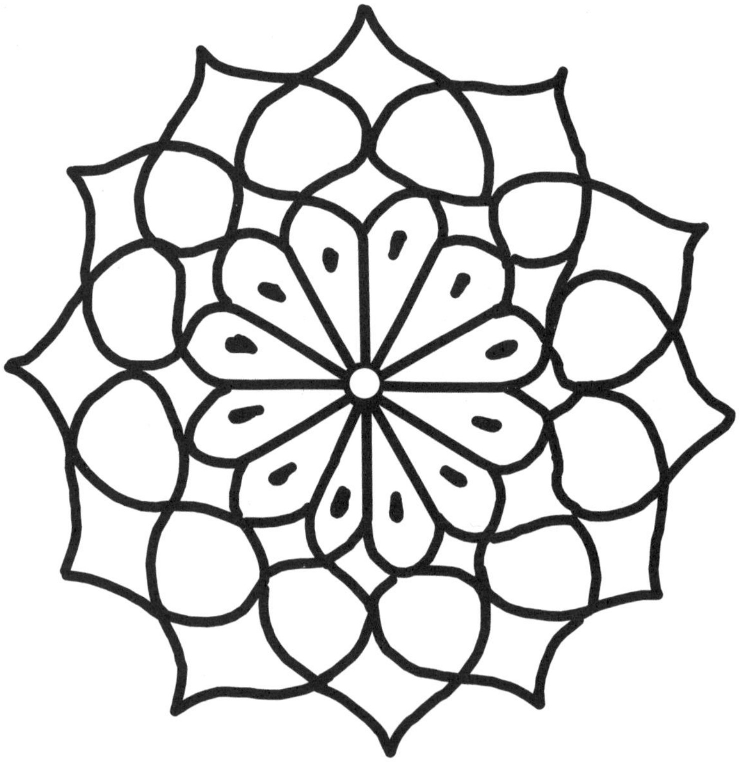

Lotus

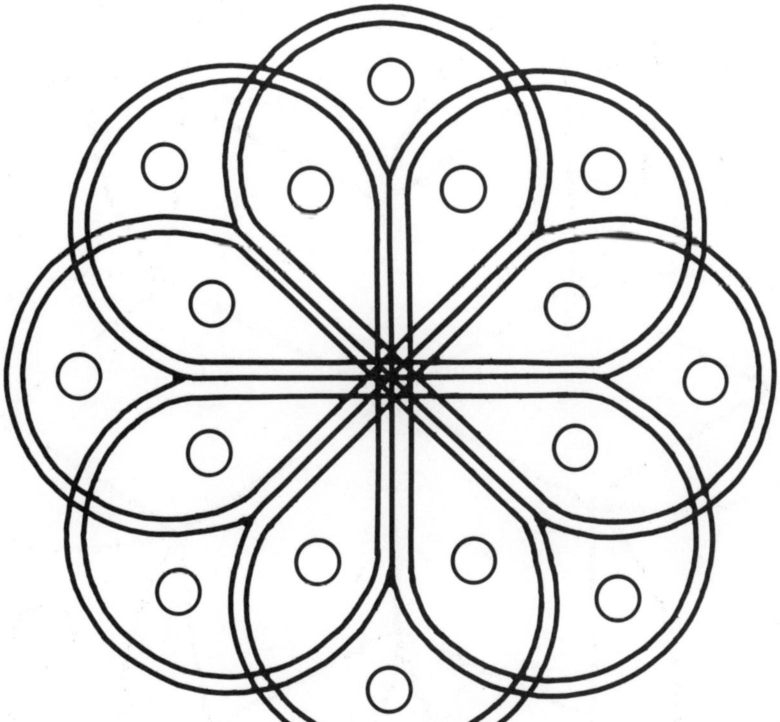



Lotus leaf

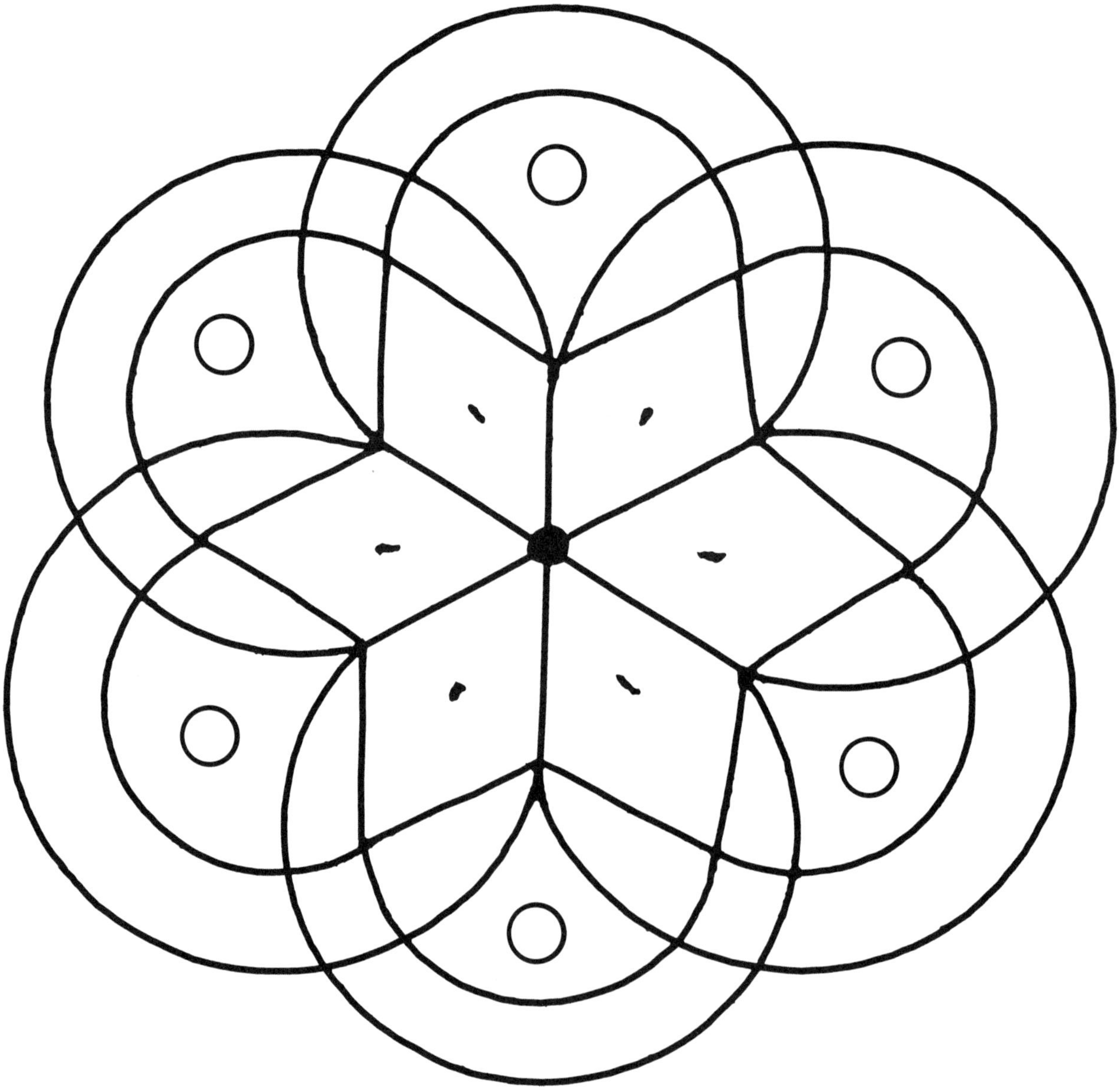

Lotus

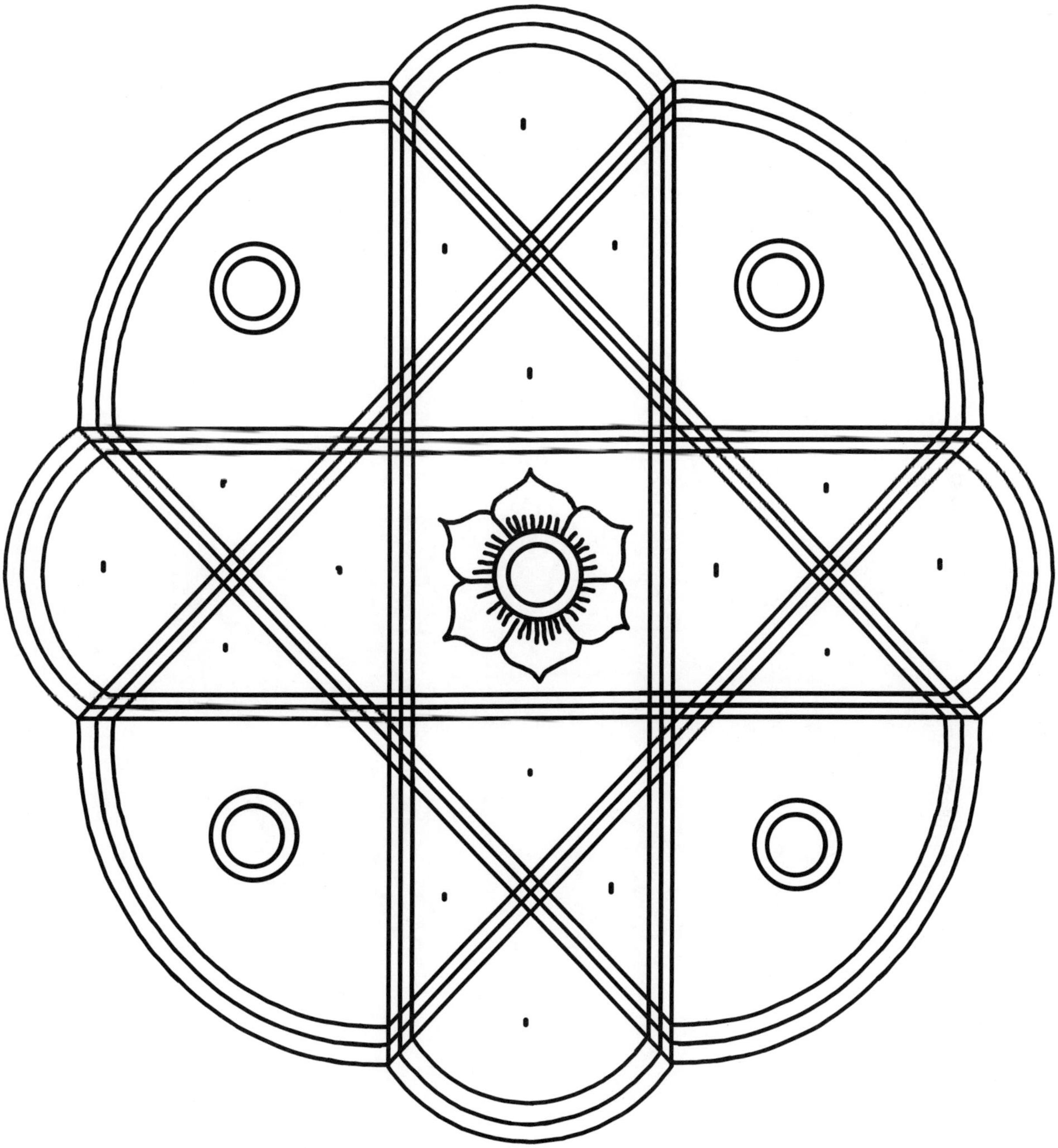



Island of Ranga

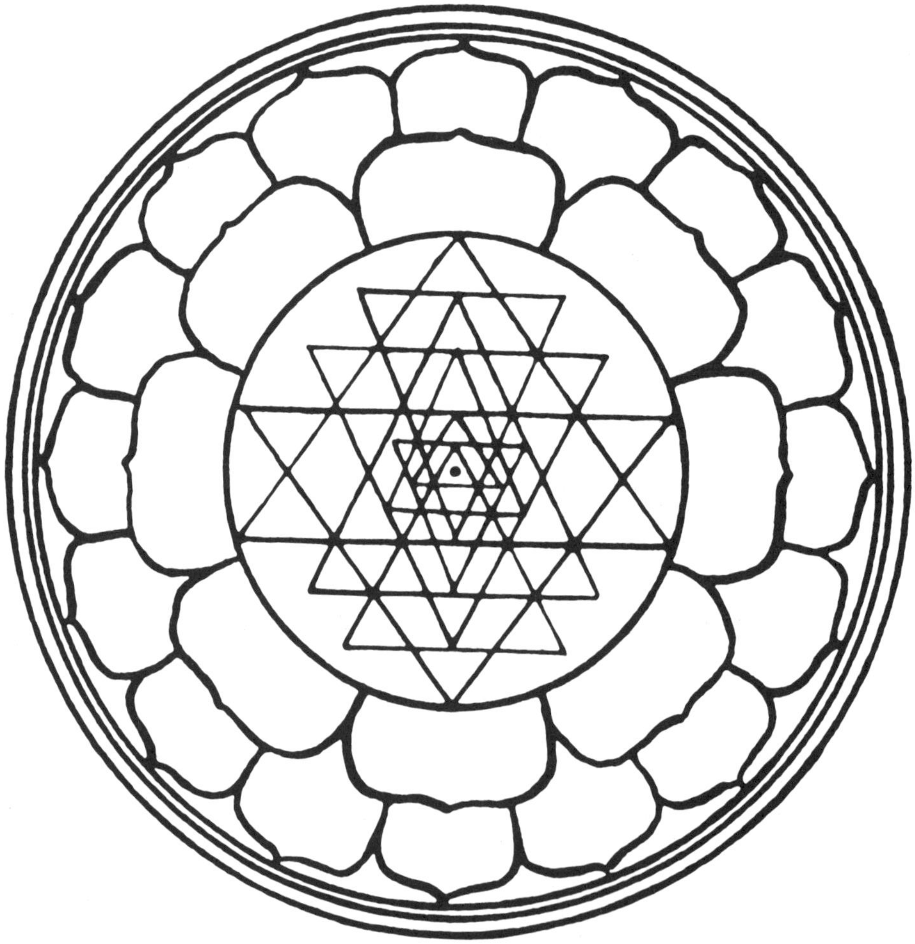



Chakram

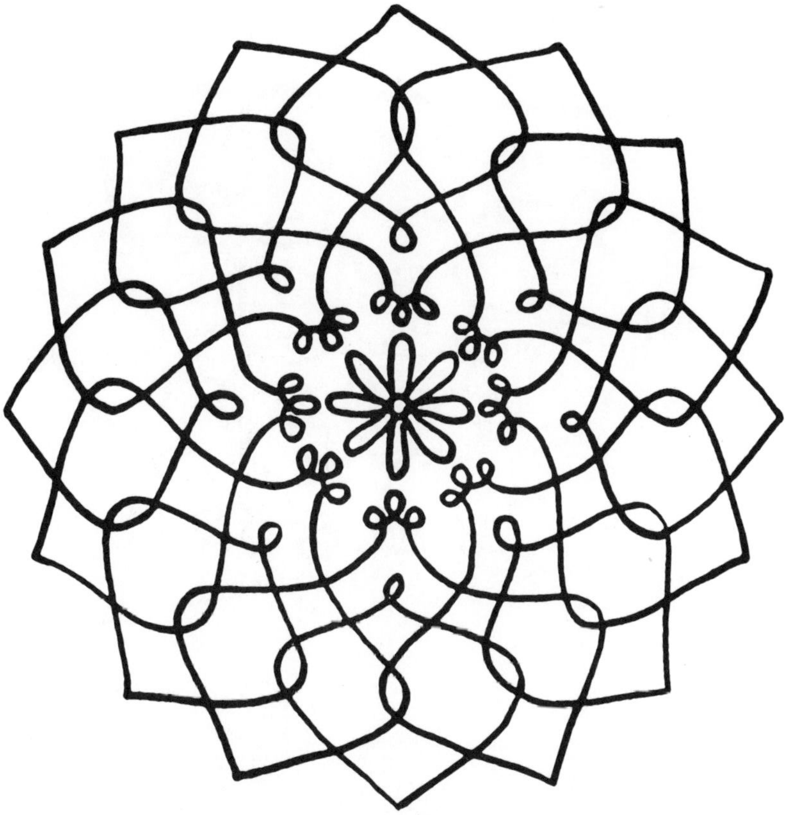

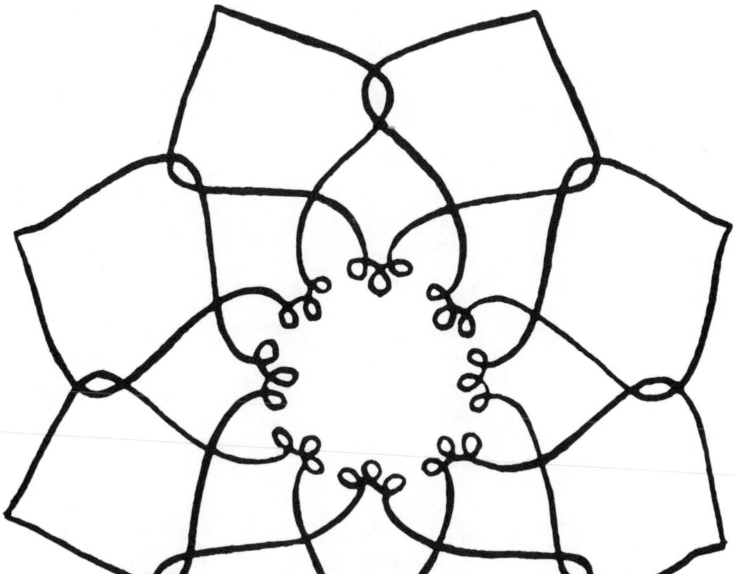



Lotus flowers

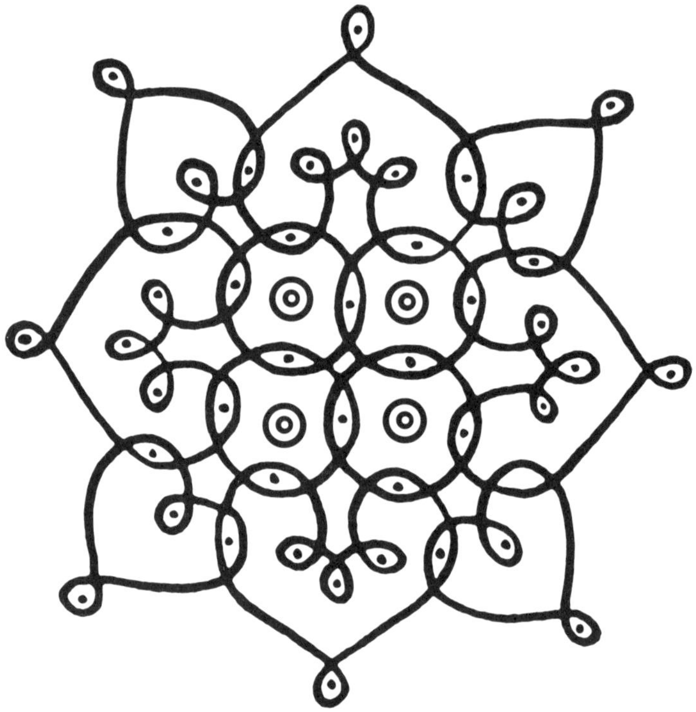

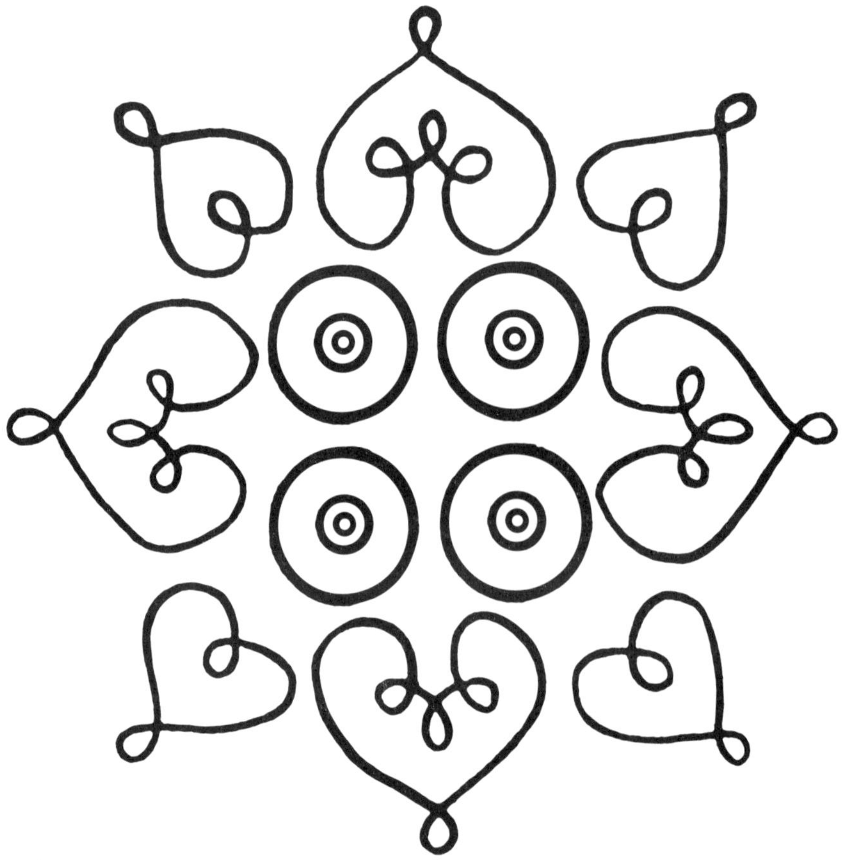

Lotus flowers

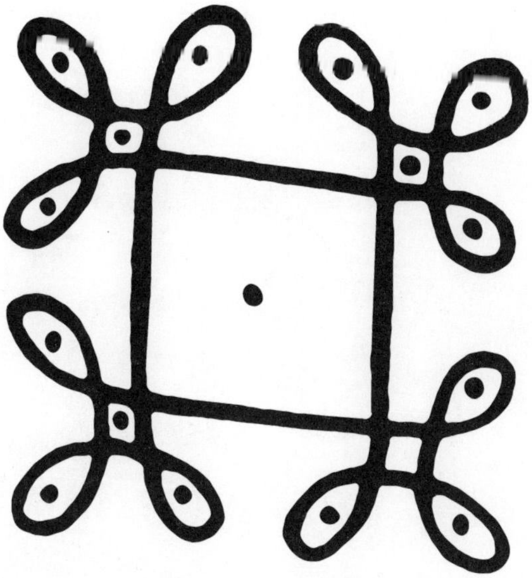



Bunch of lemons

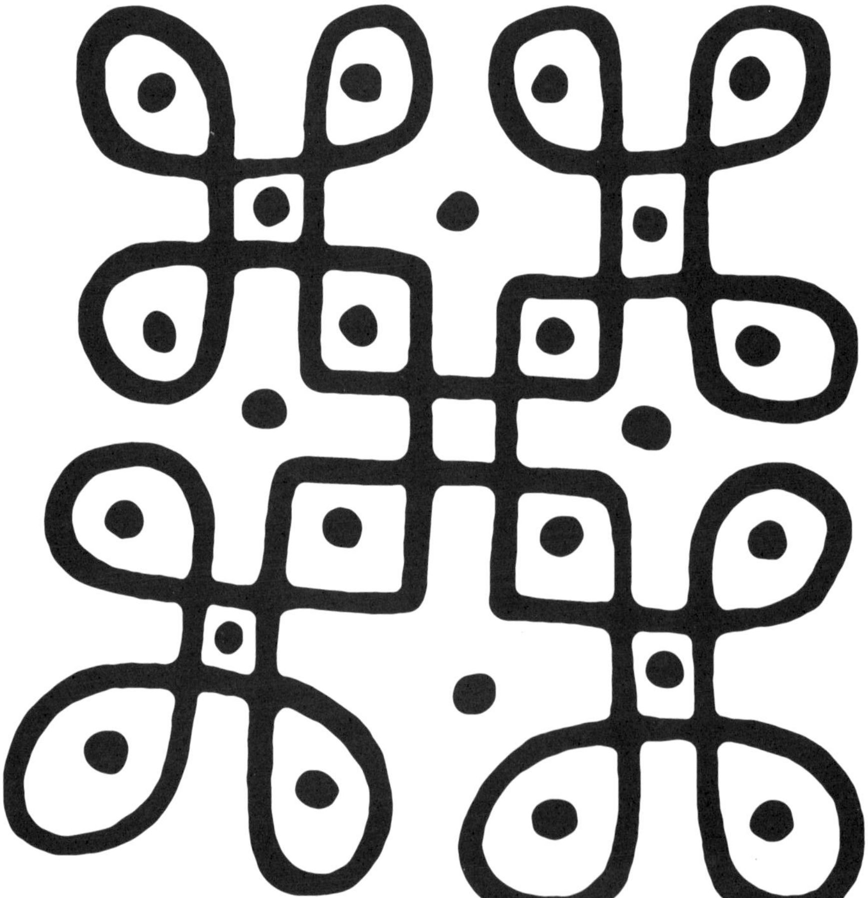

Bunch of limes

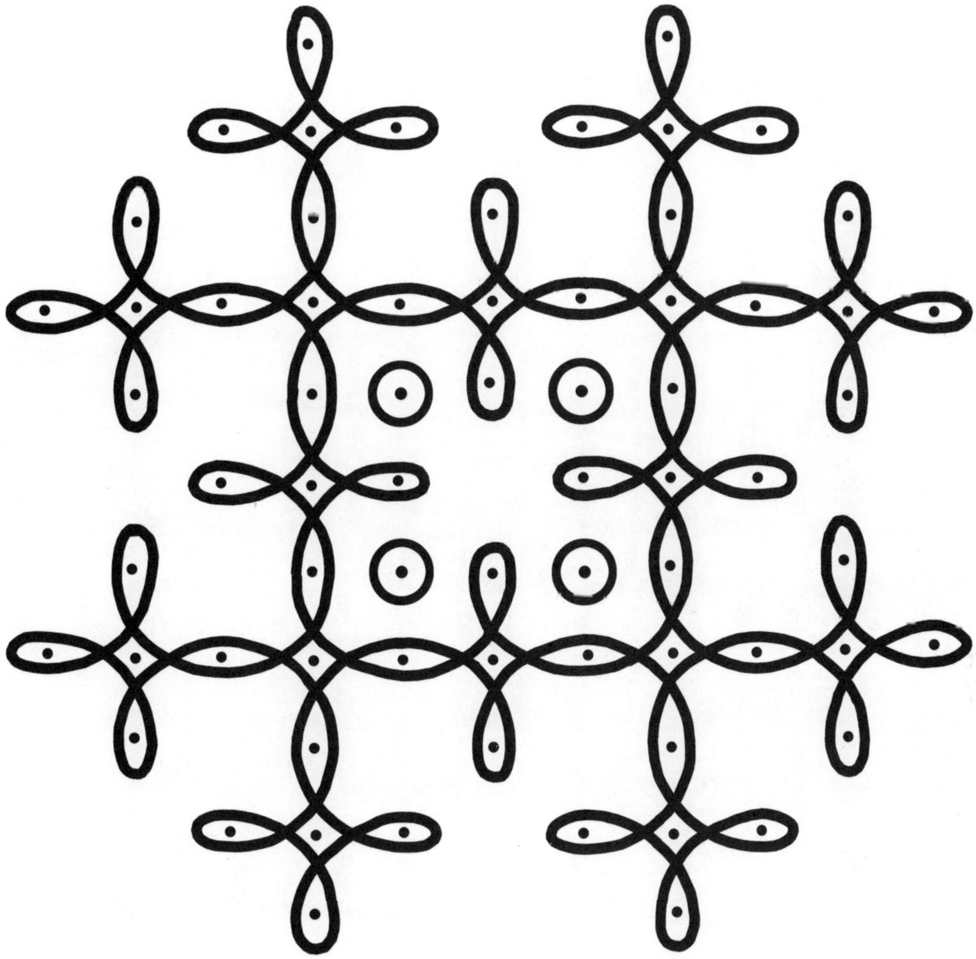

Bunch of lemons

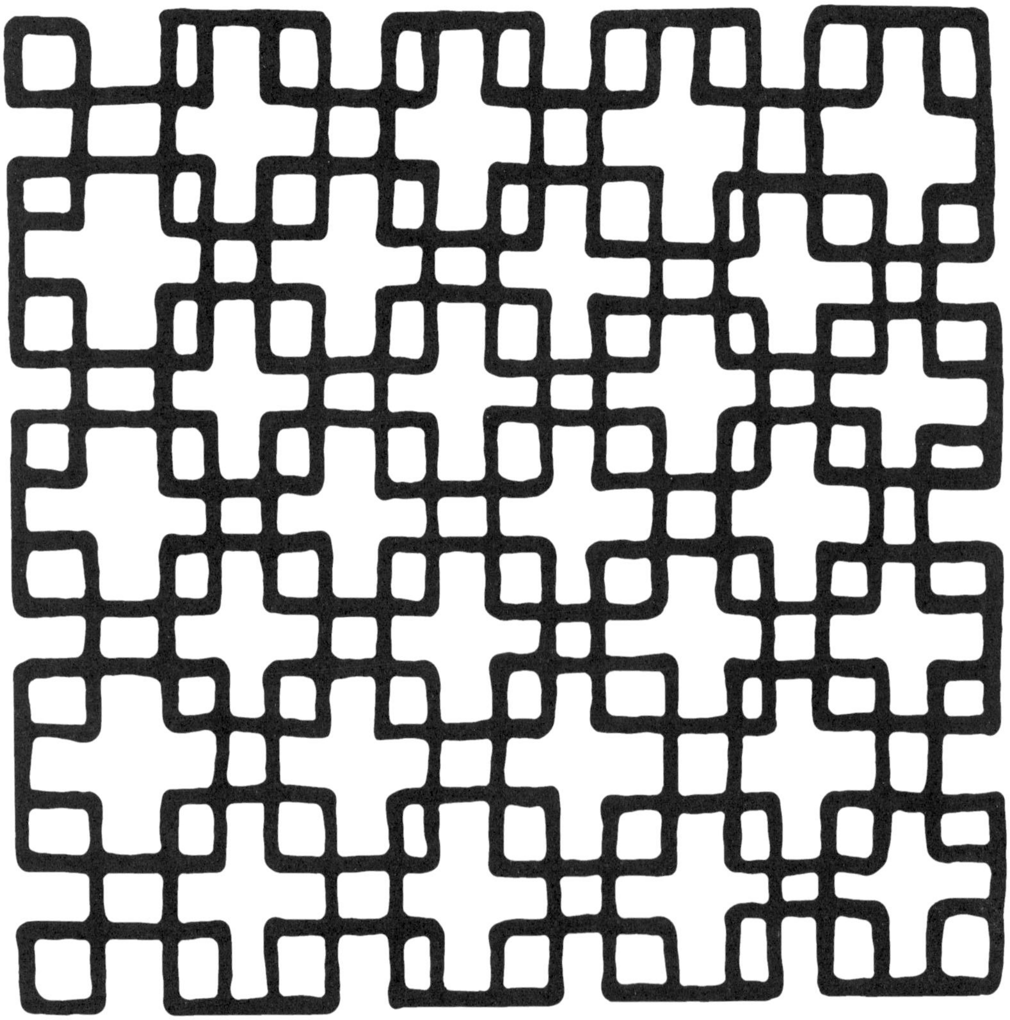



Unknown design

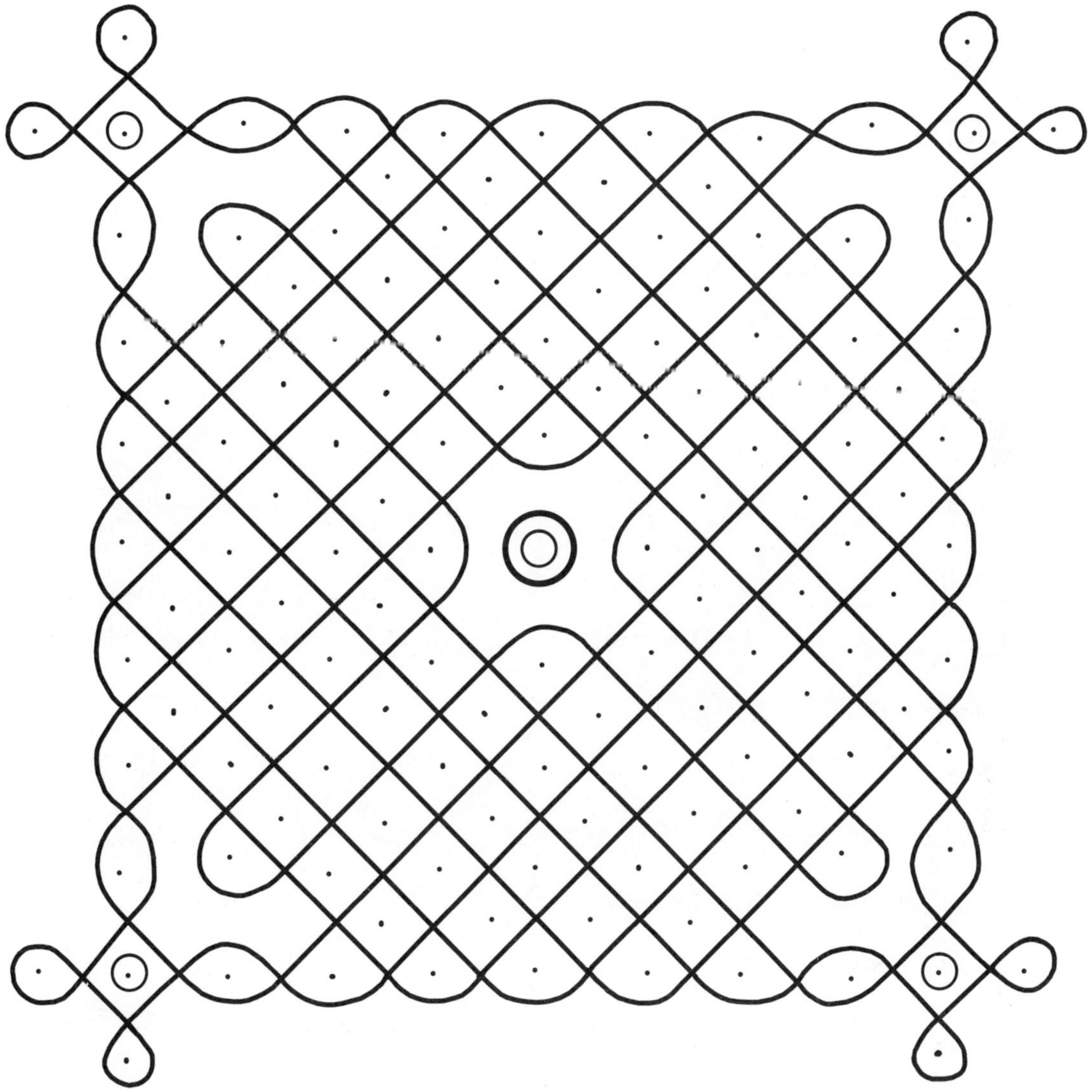



Cradle

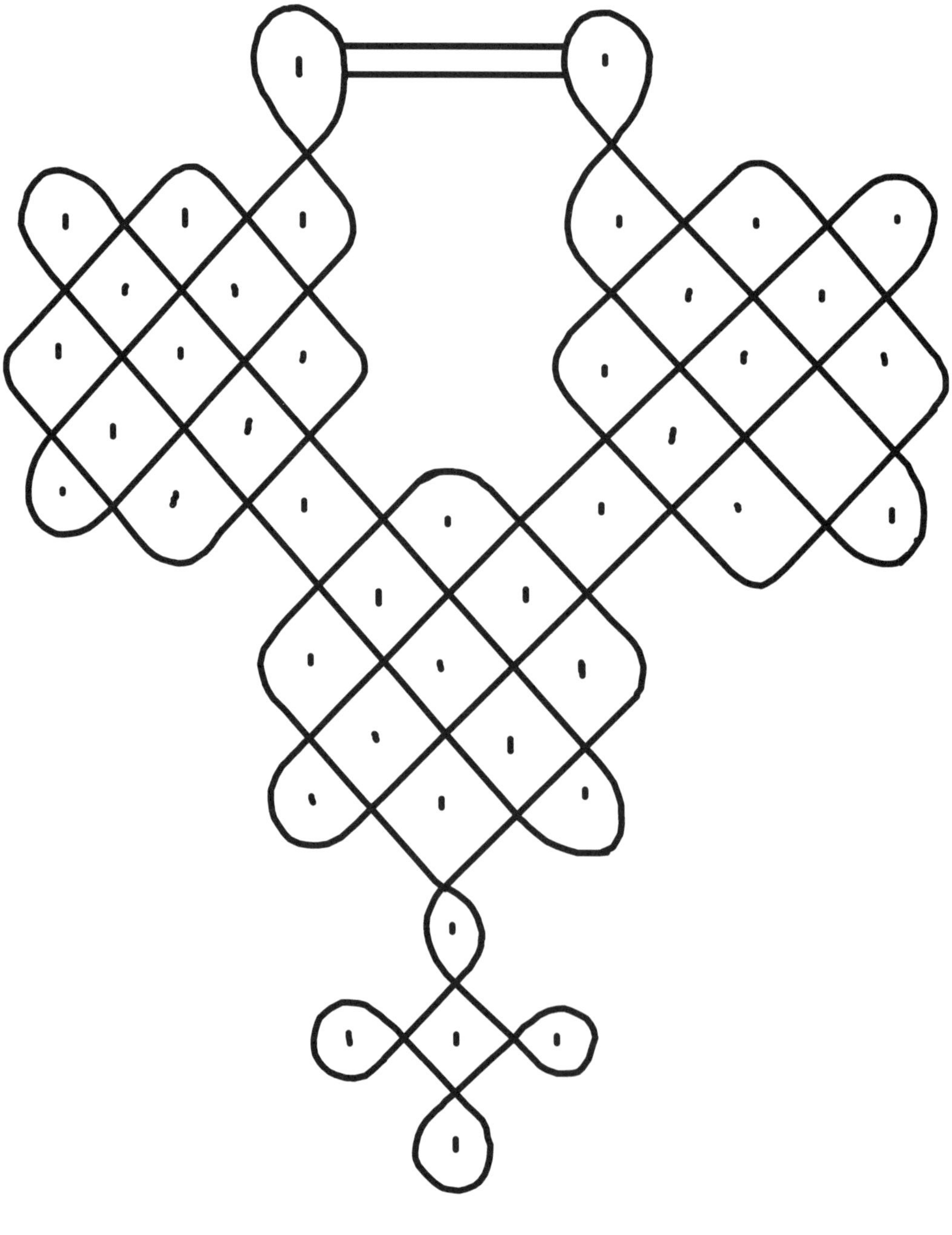

Nose jewel

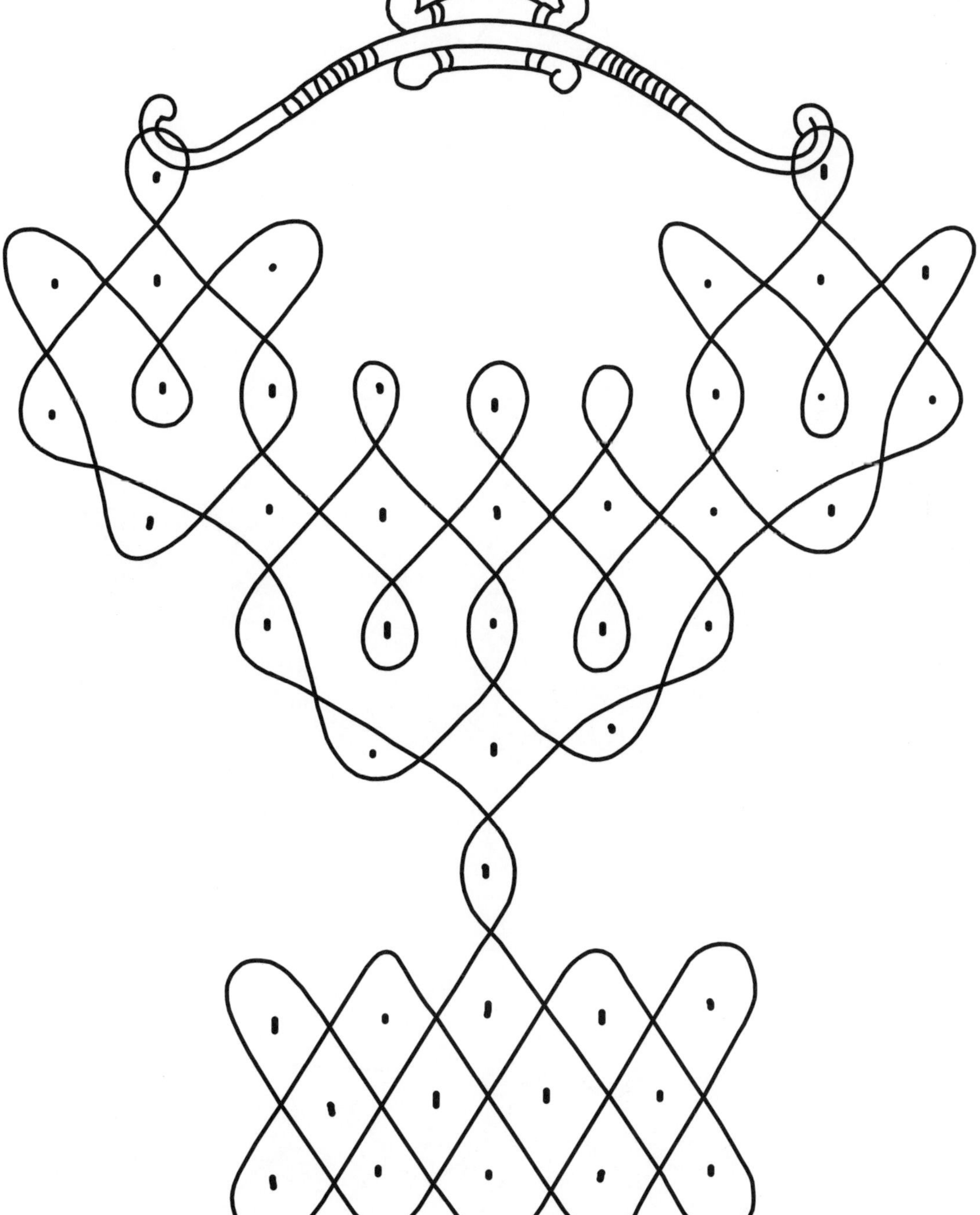



Nose jewel

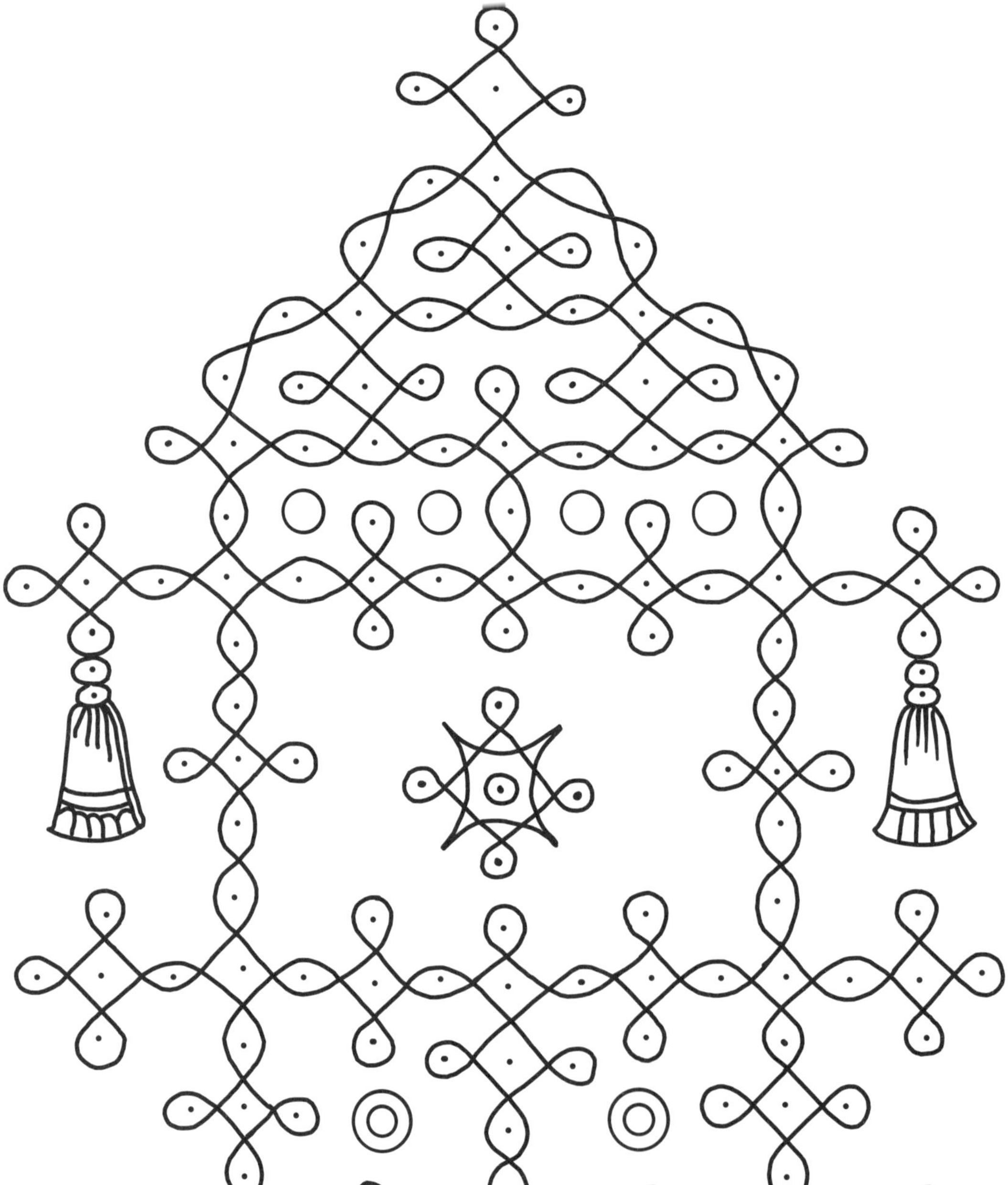

Flying chariot

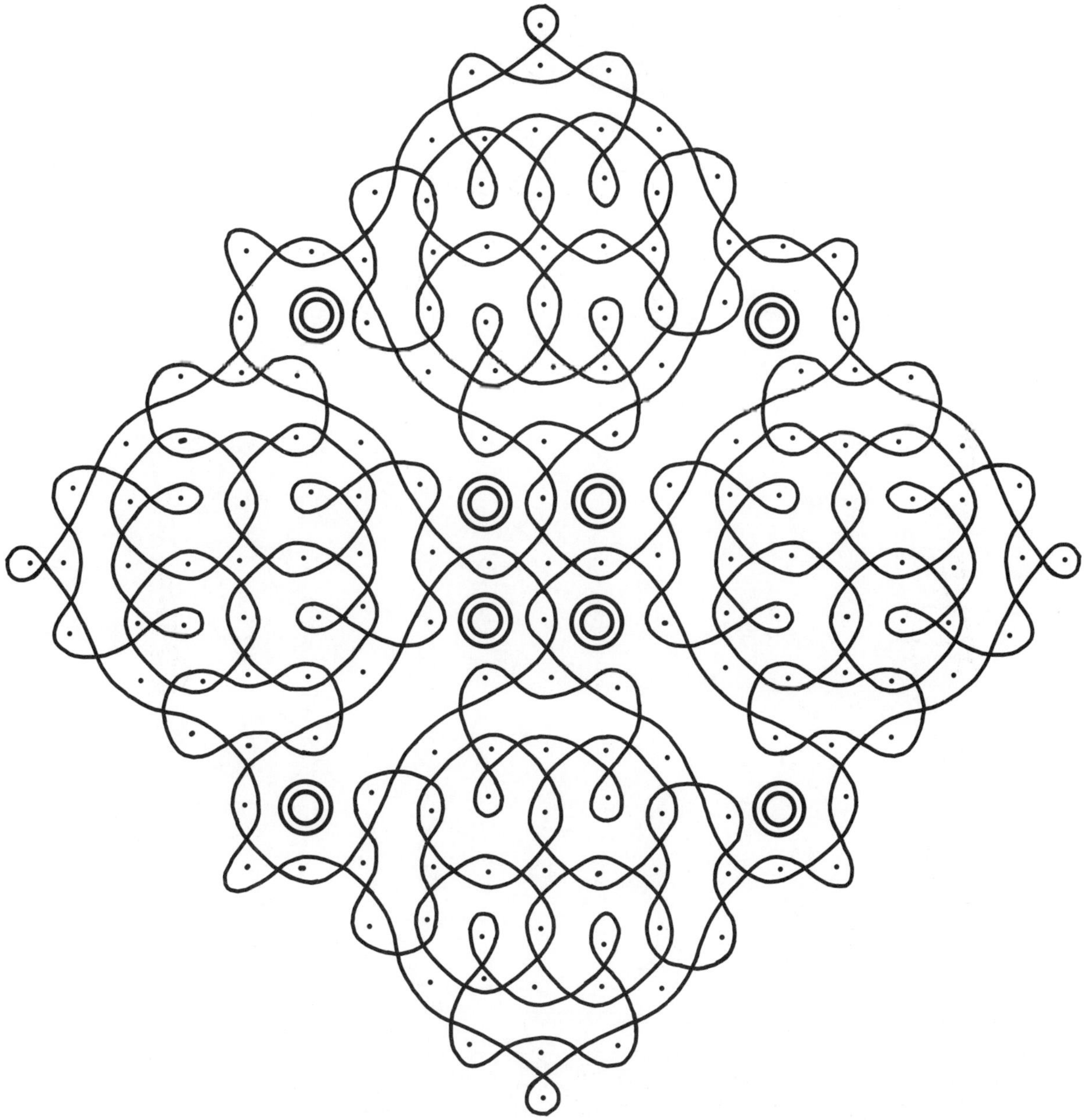



Brahma's hair

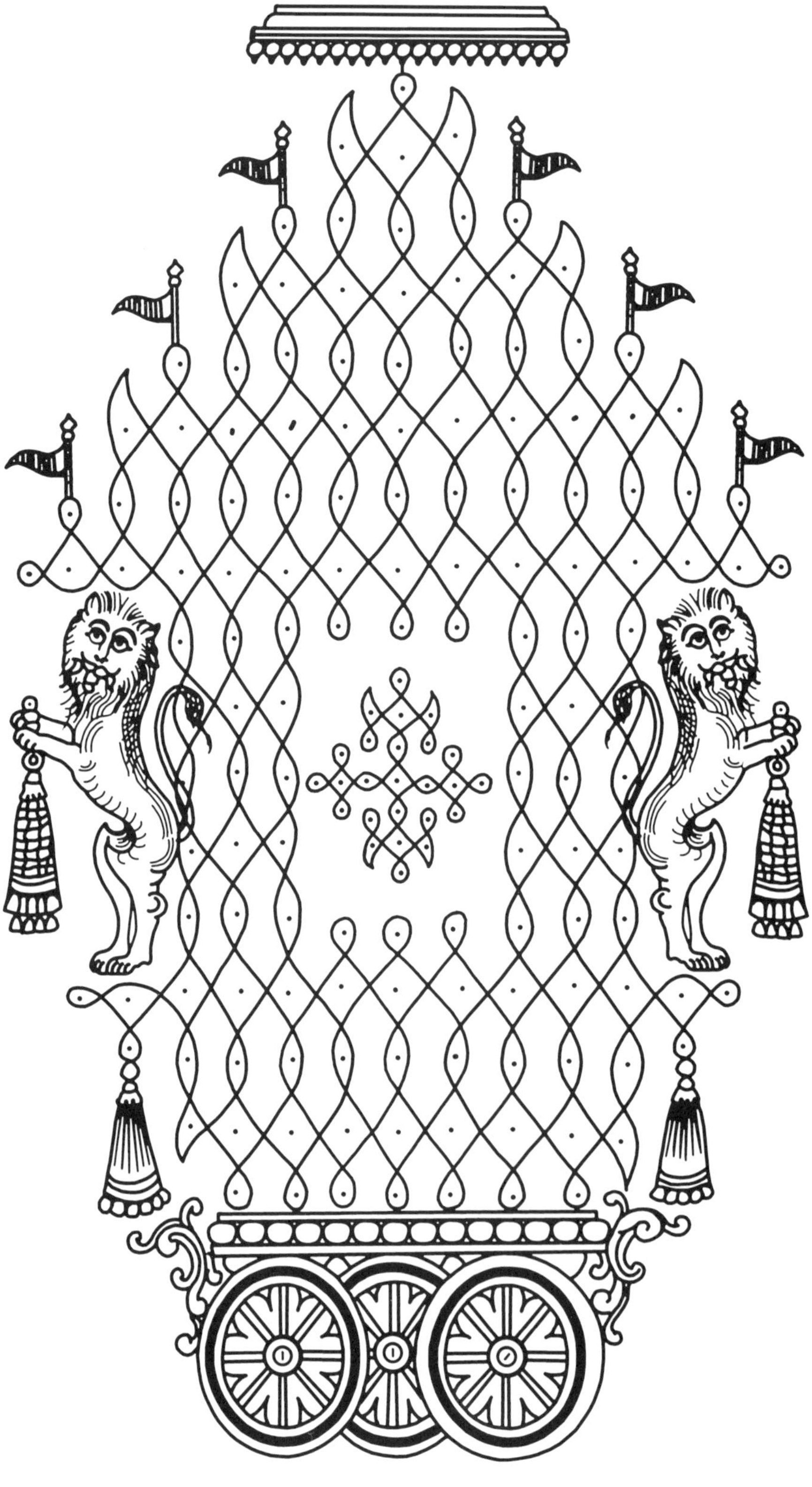

Chariot of flowers

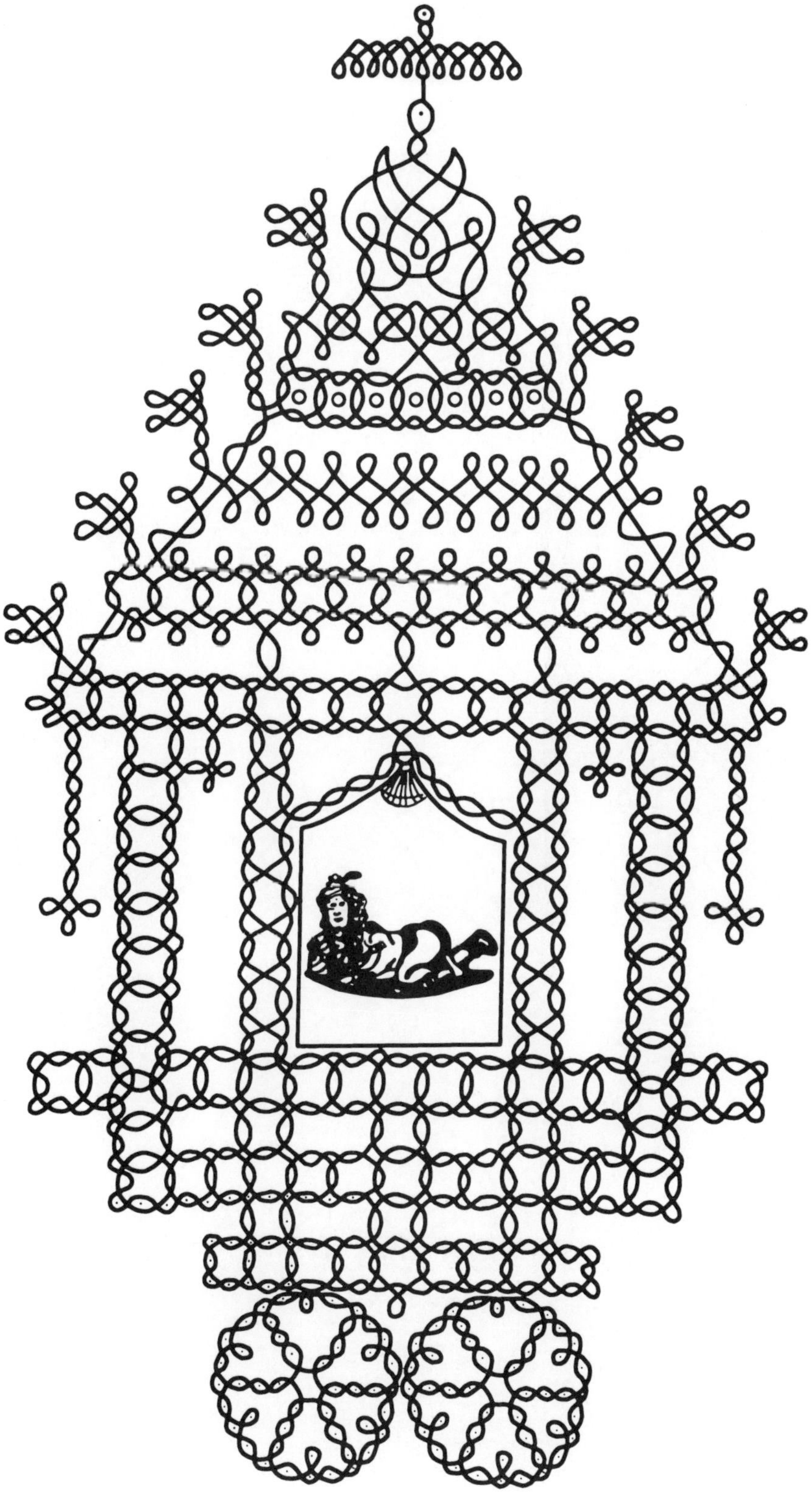

Chariot

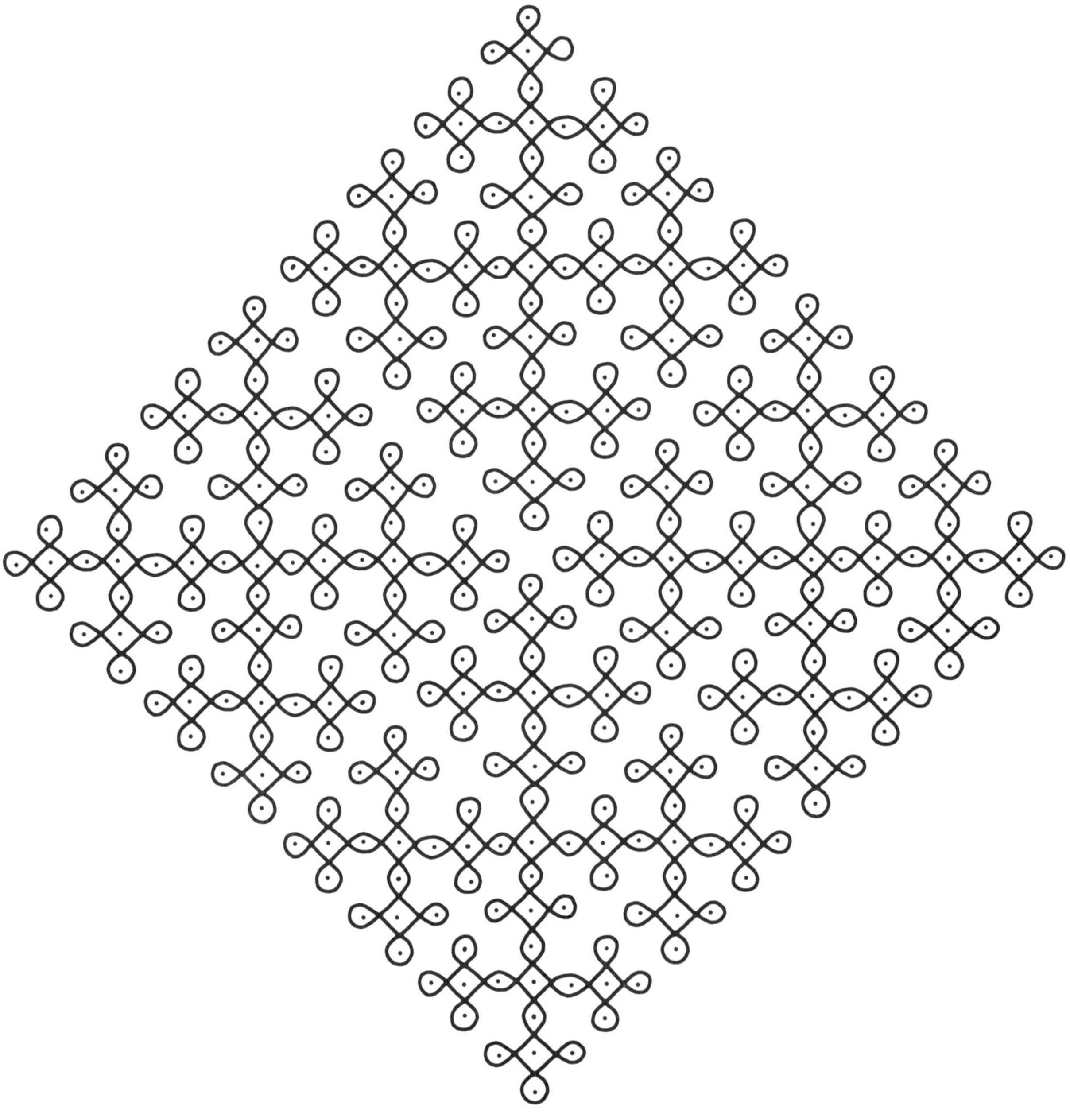



Bunch of lemons

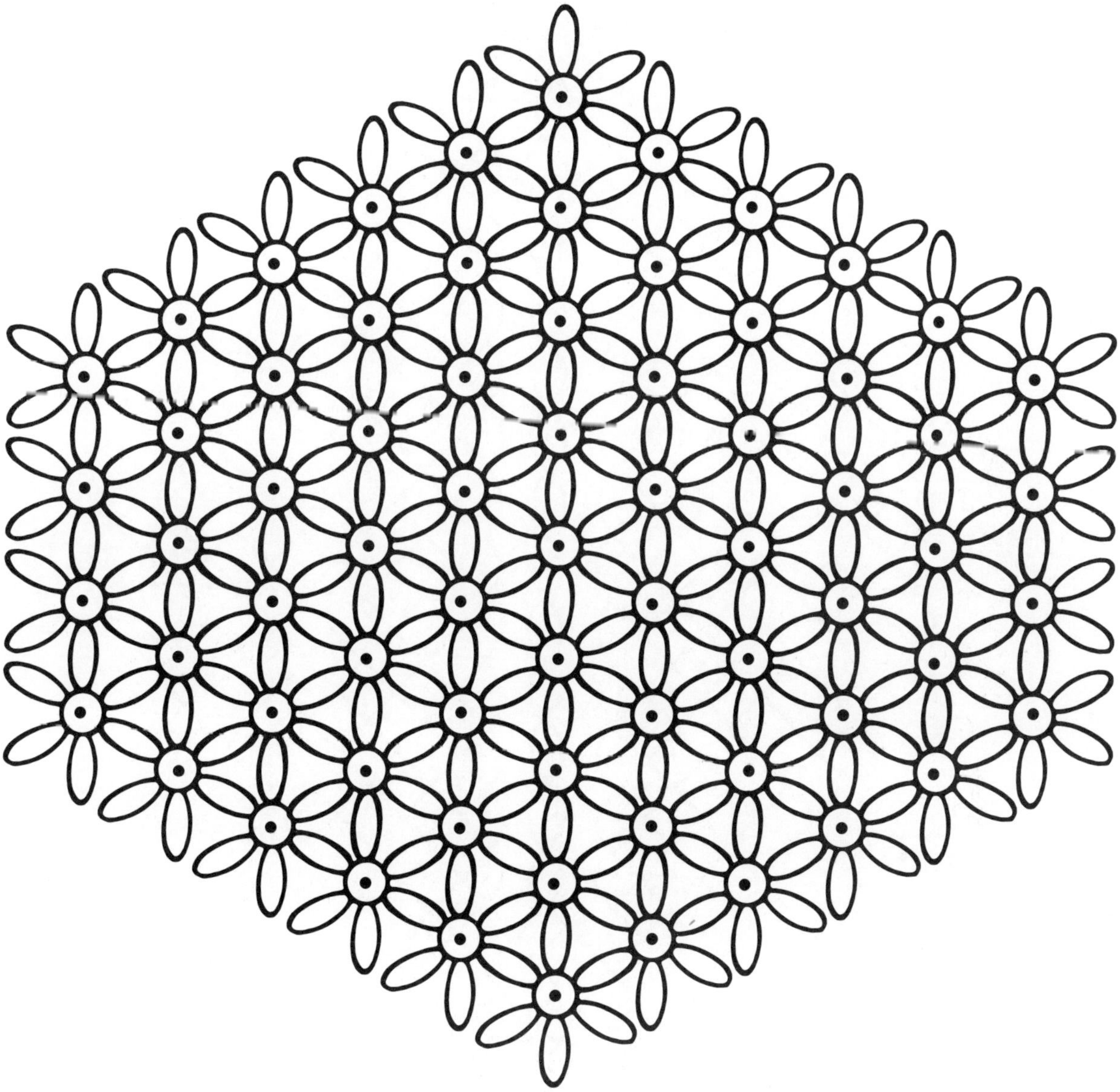



Bunch of pineapples

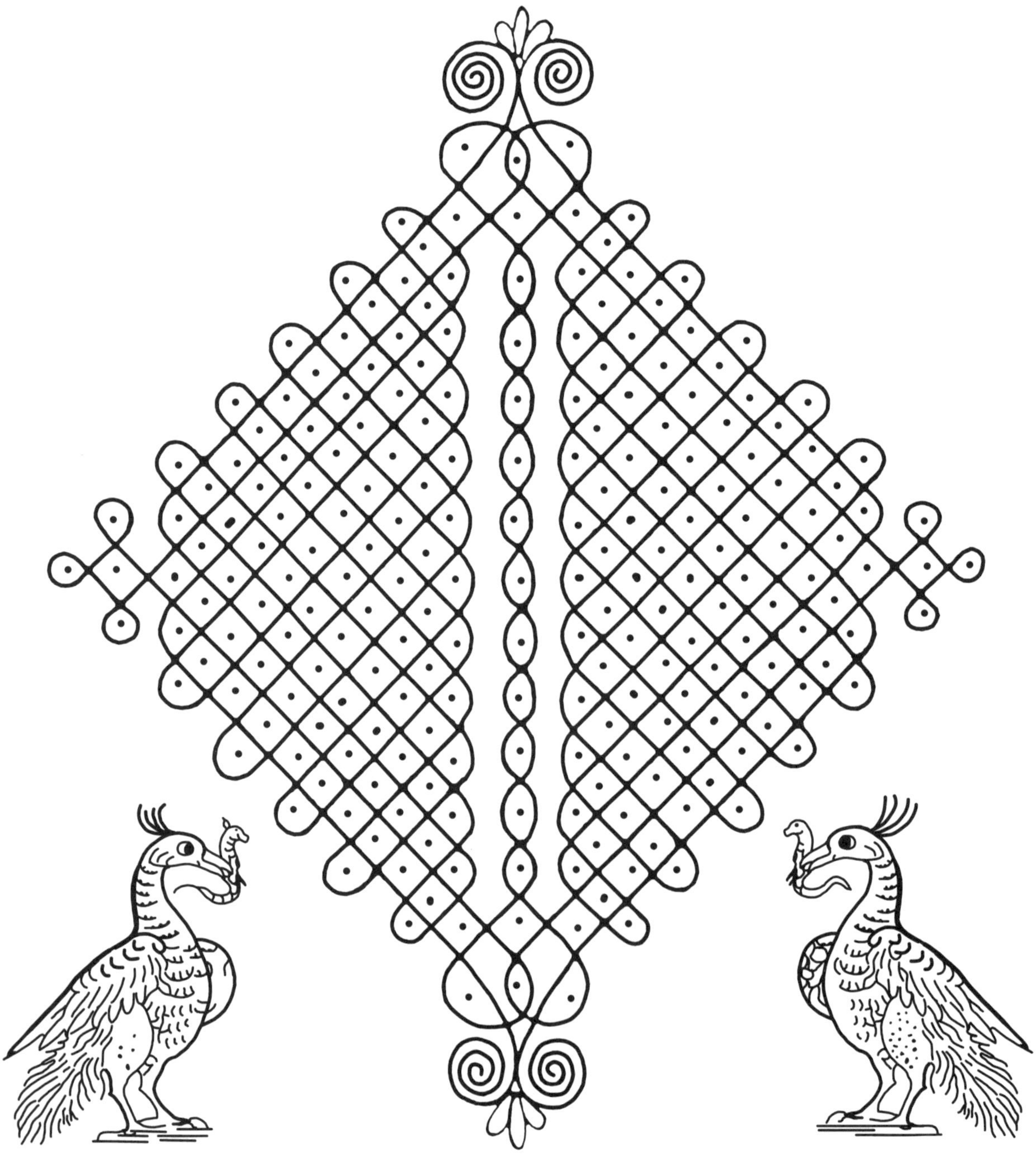

Stream of water

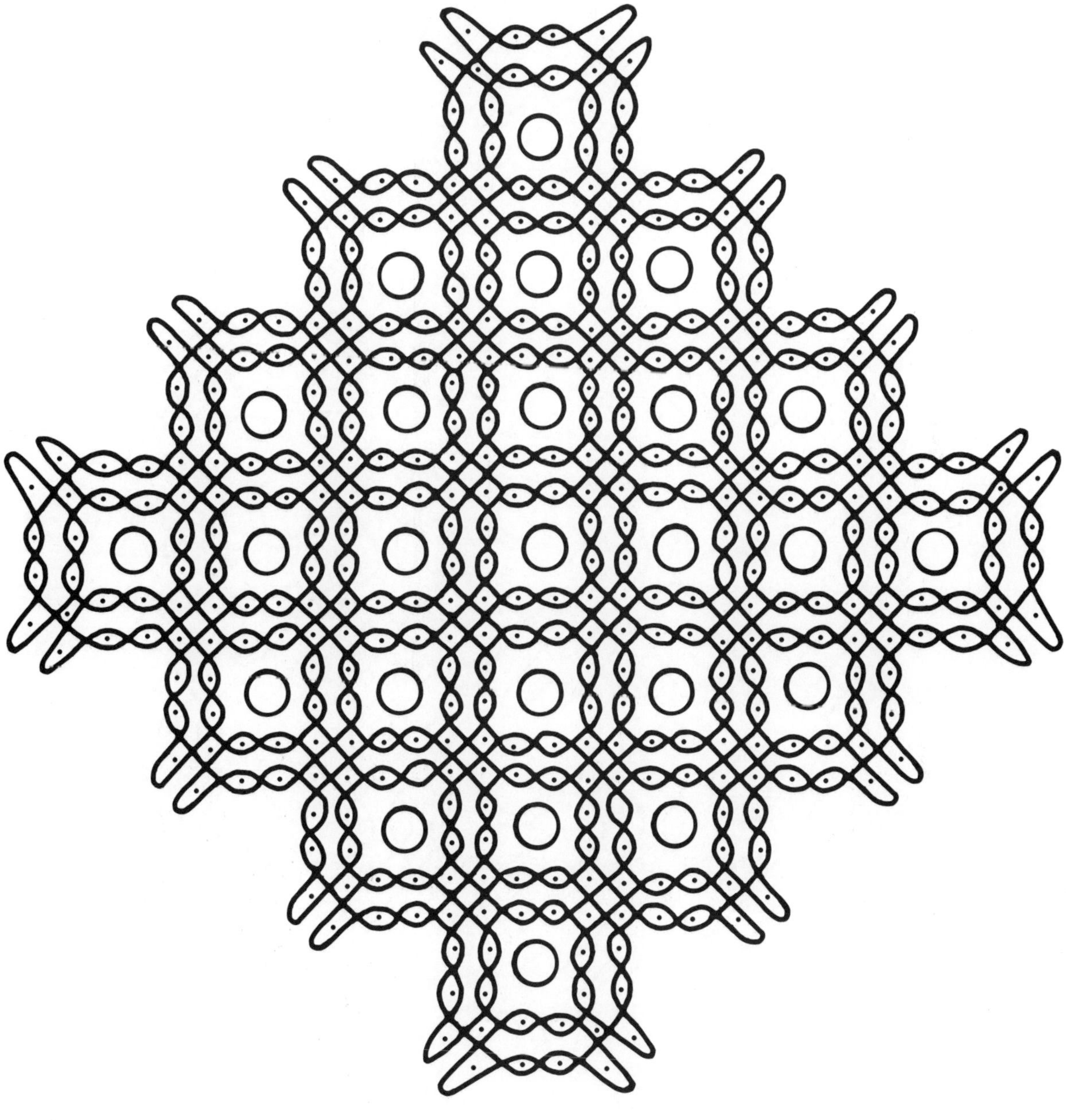

Elephant's foot

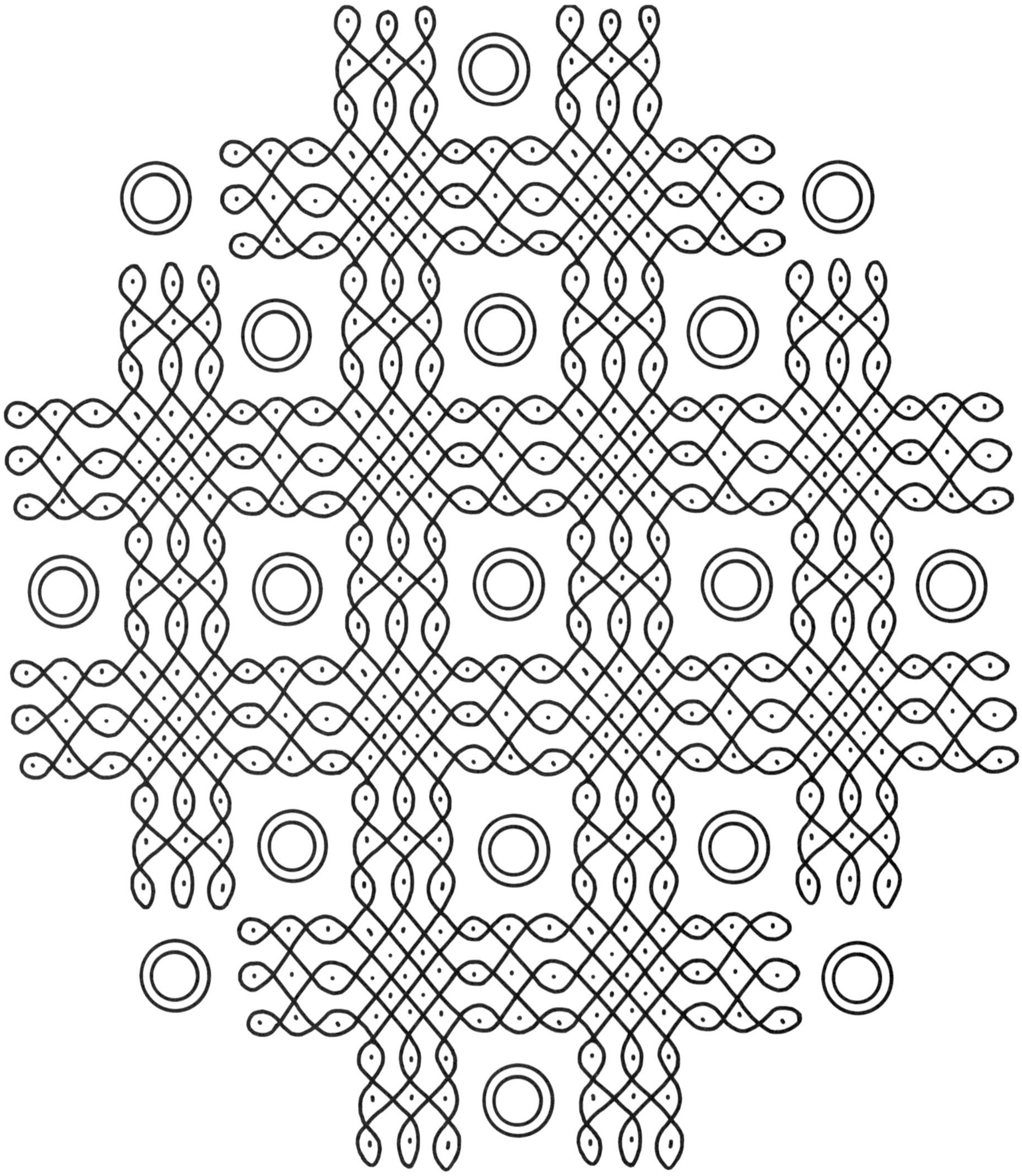



Pantal

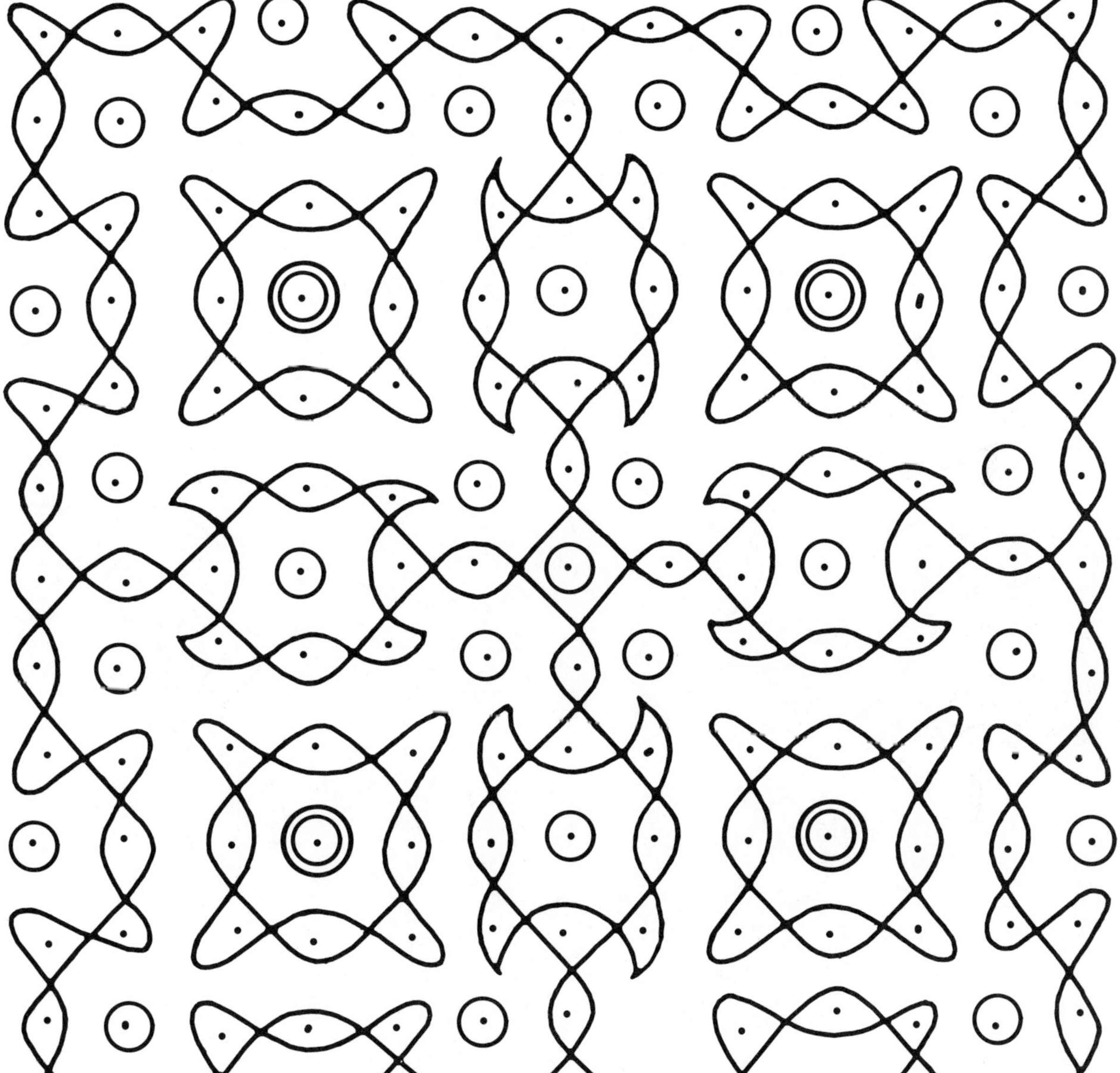



Angled pattern

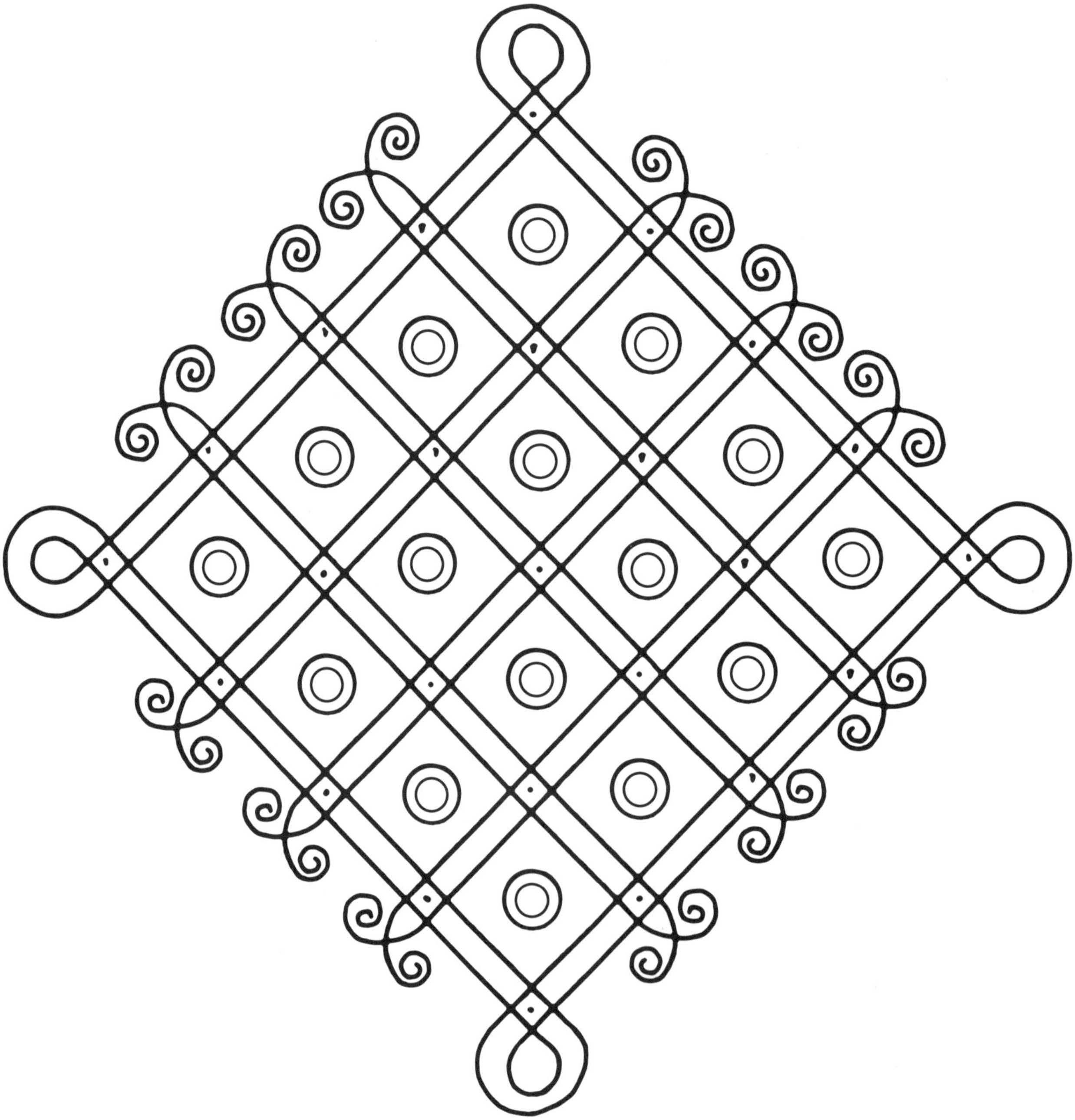



Cradle

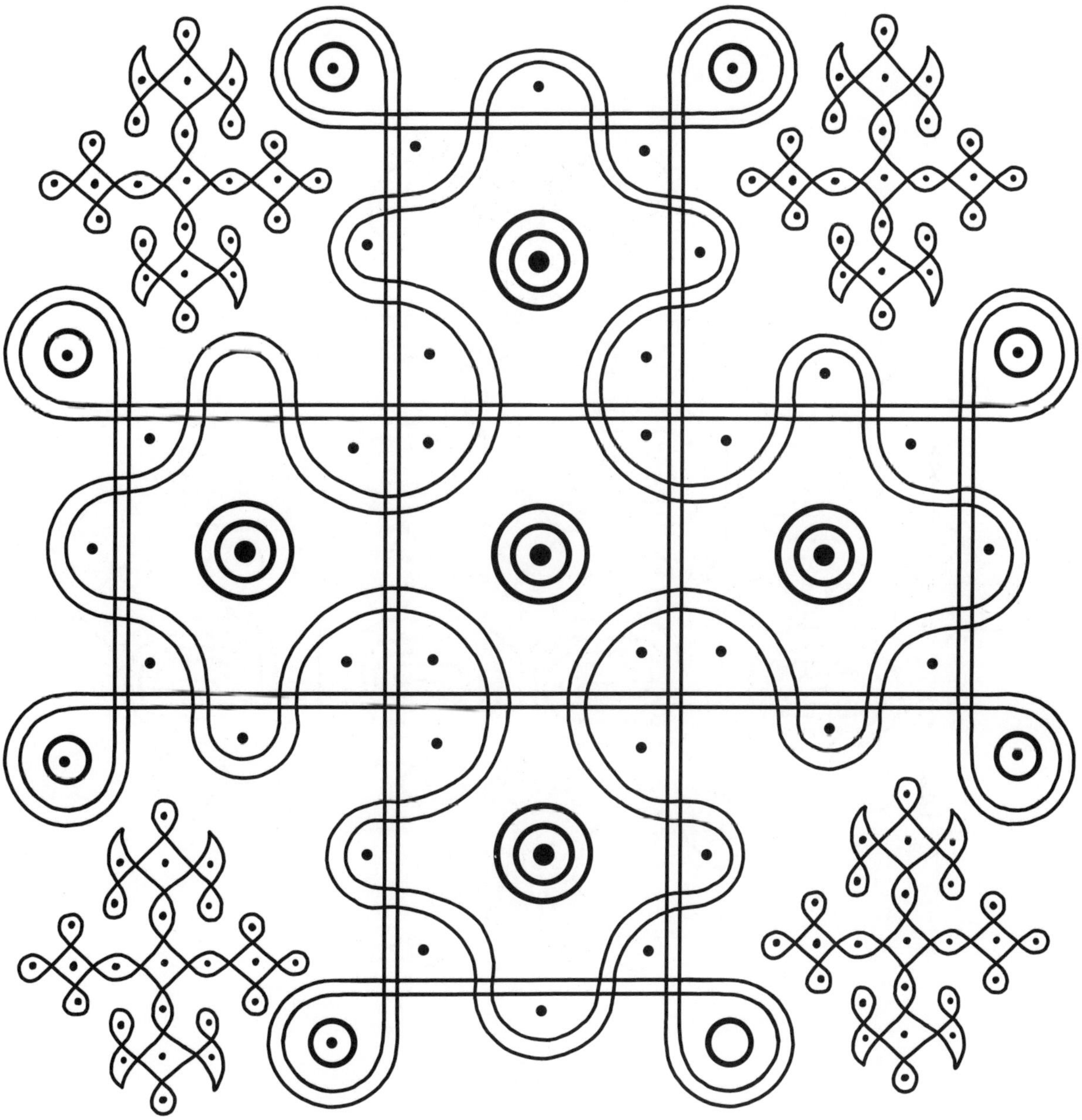



Cradle

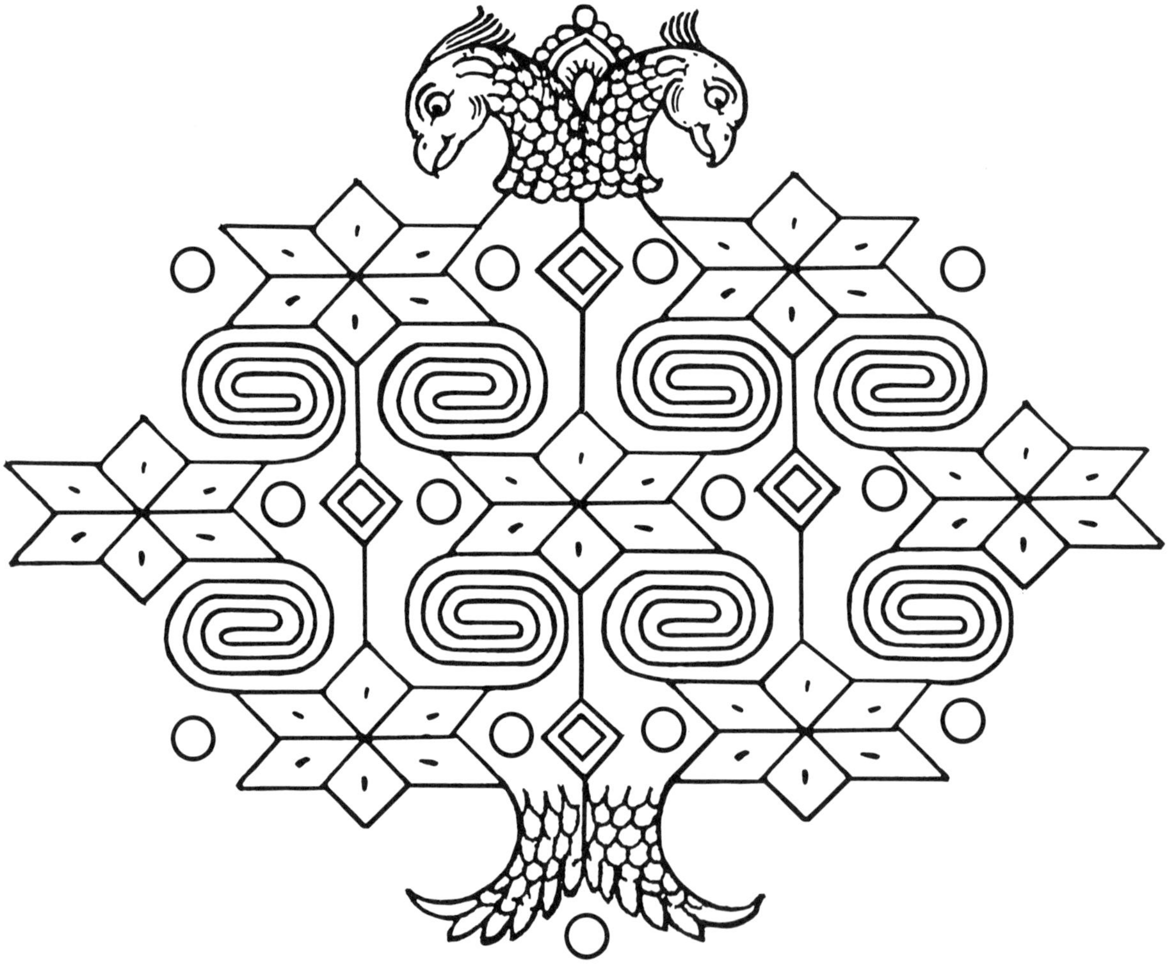



Twin bird

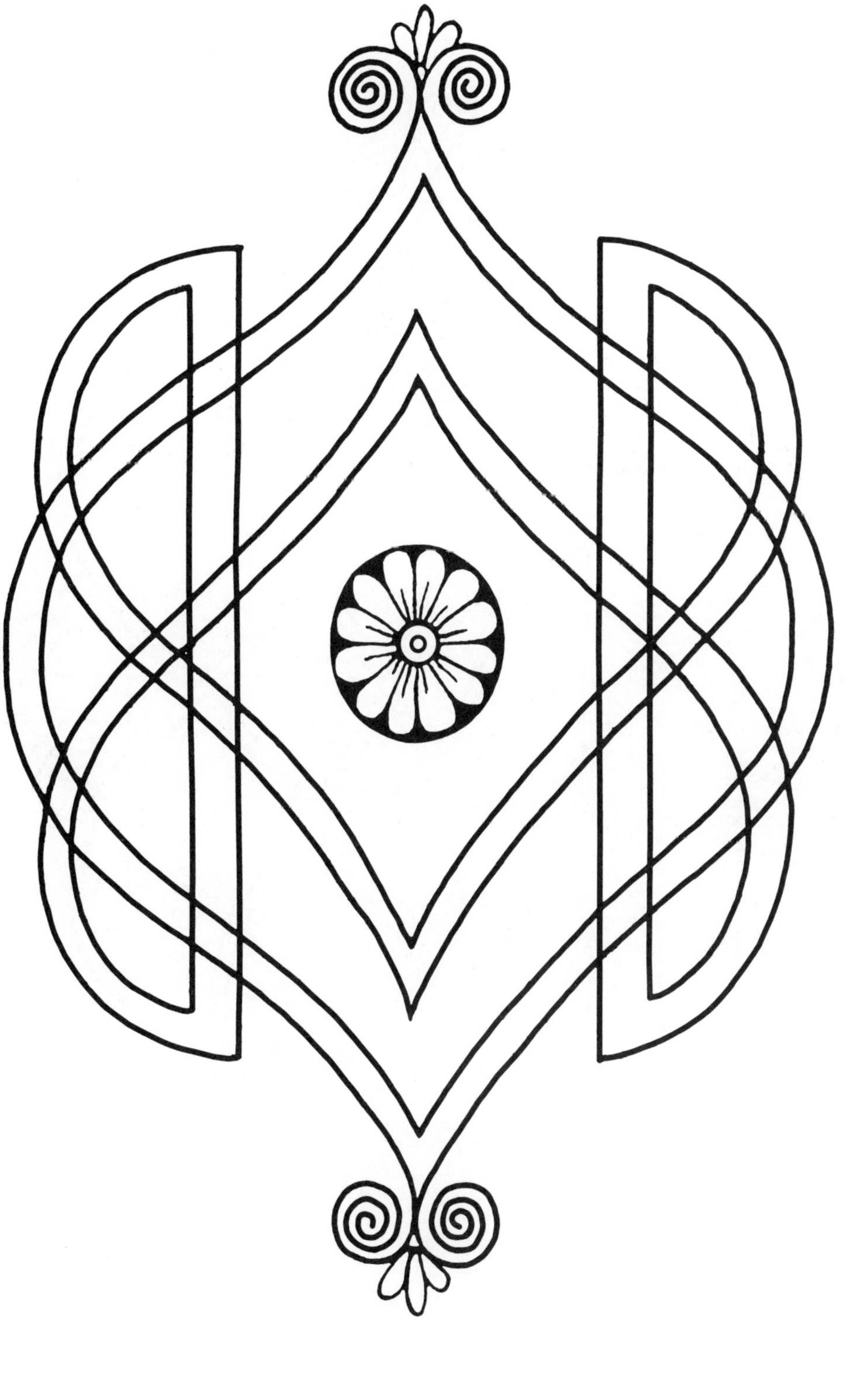



Talisman

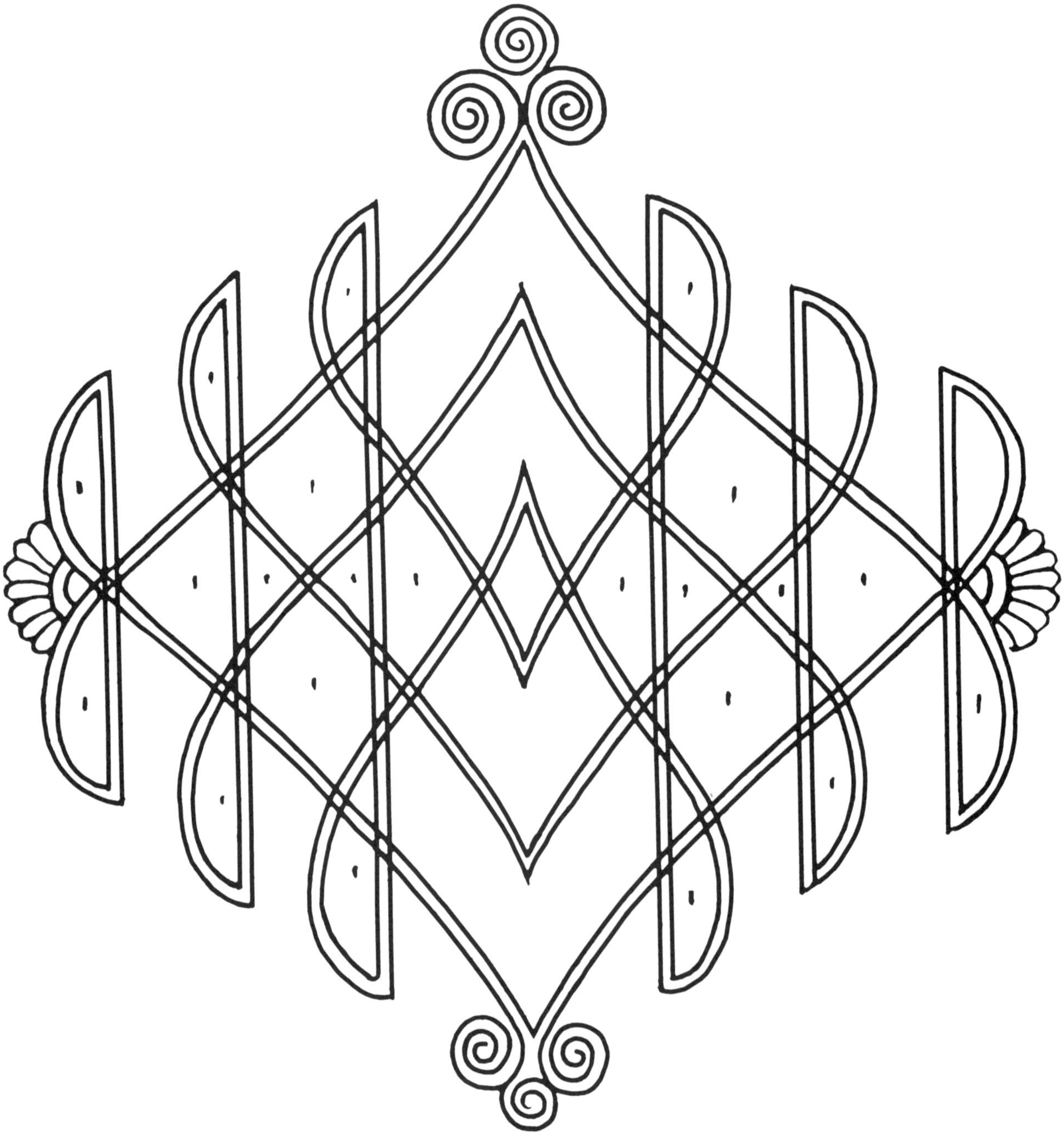



Talisman

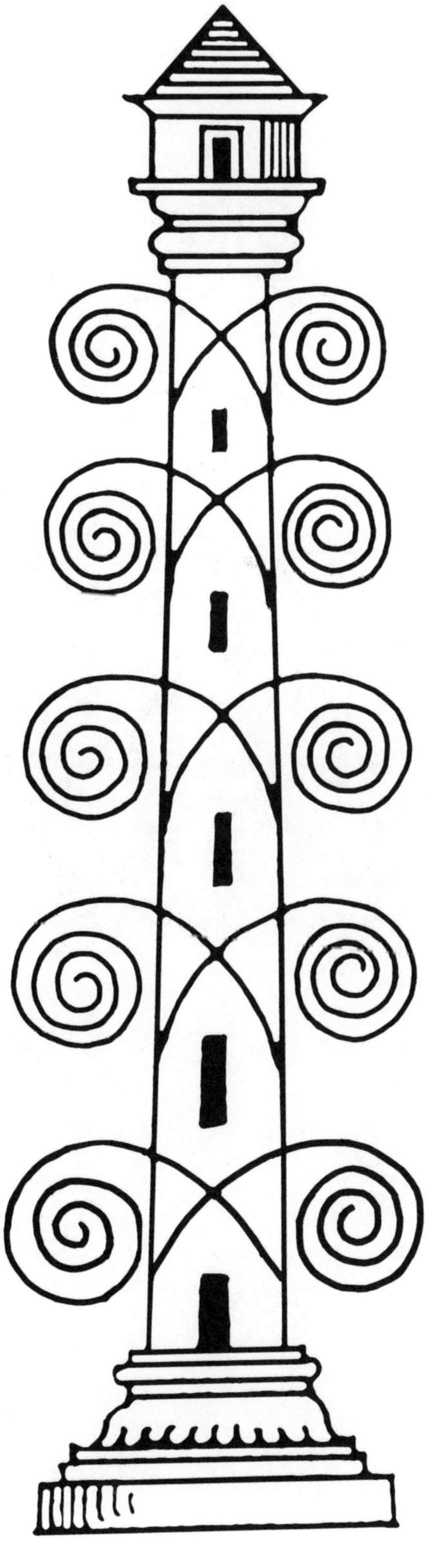



Lighthouse

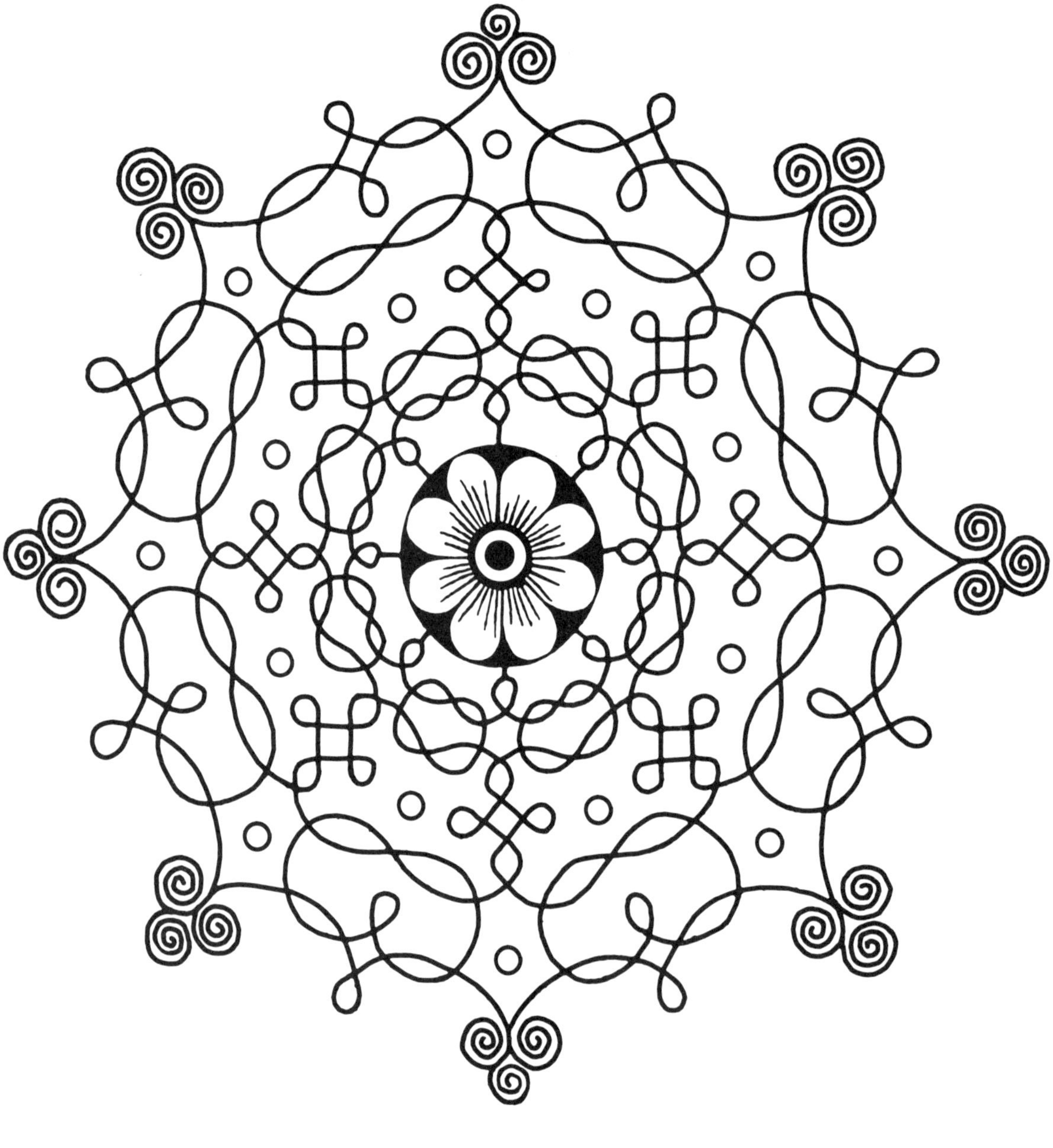

Leaf with a pattern

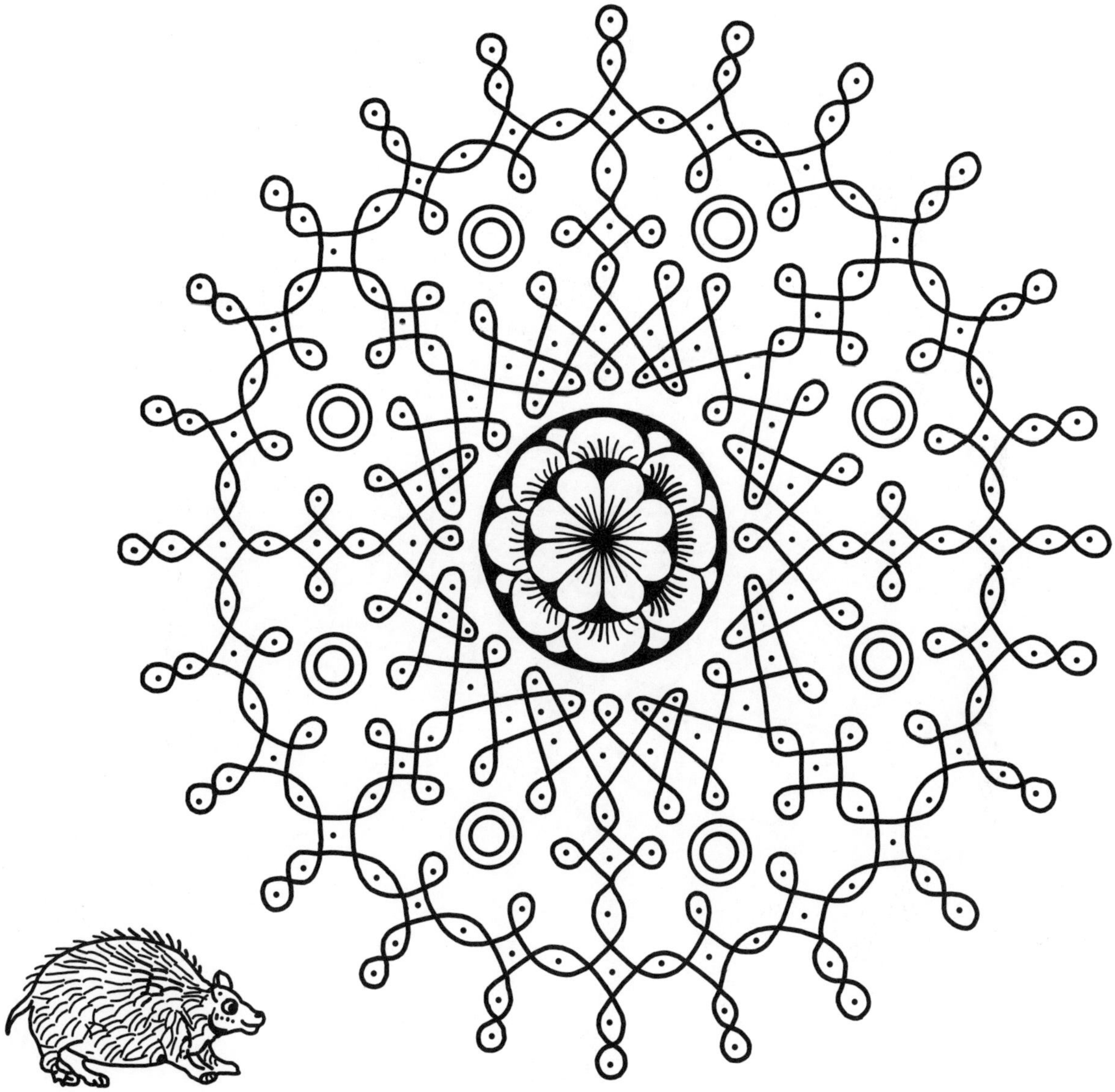



Tray with designs

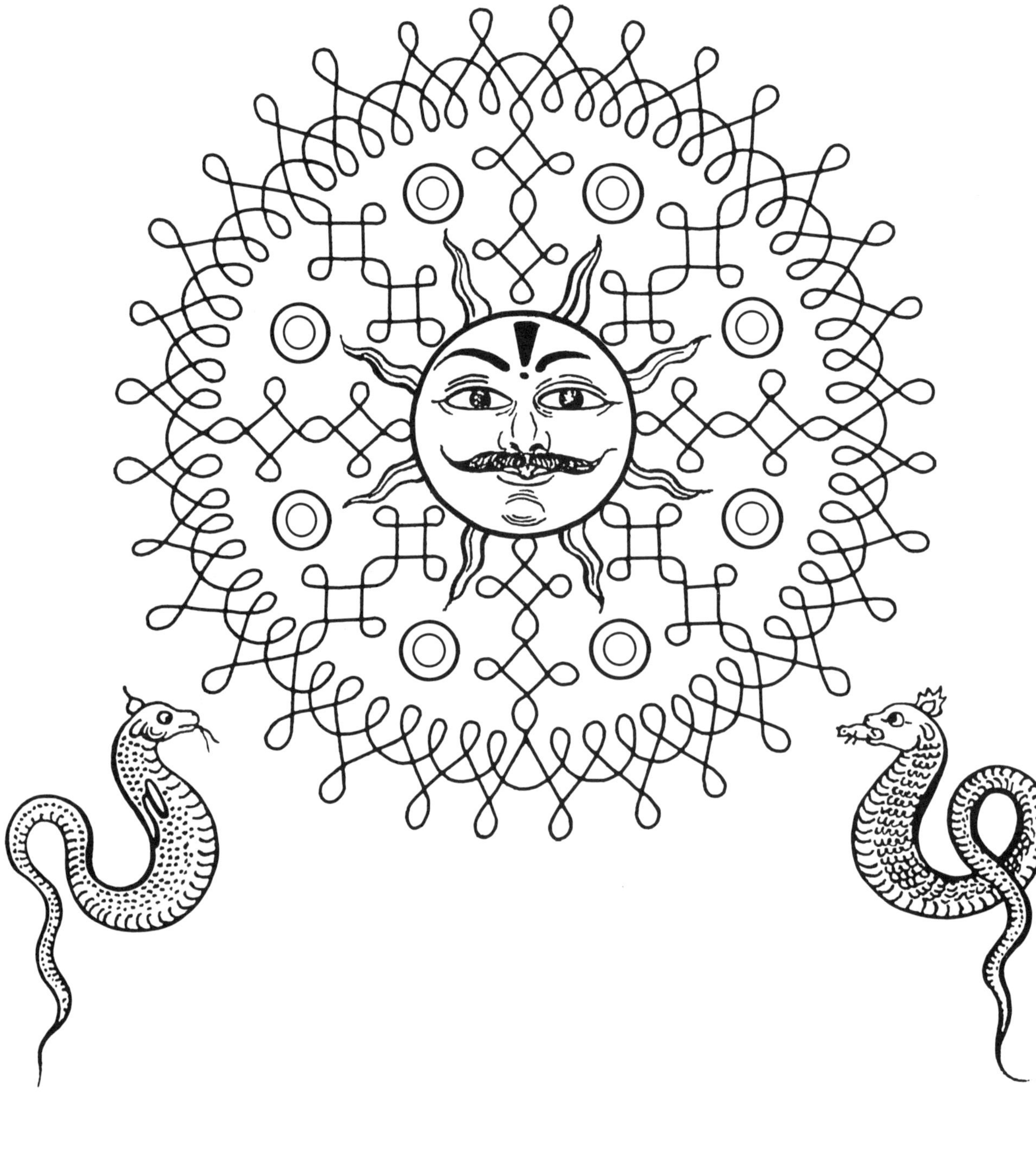

Sun

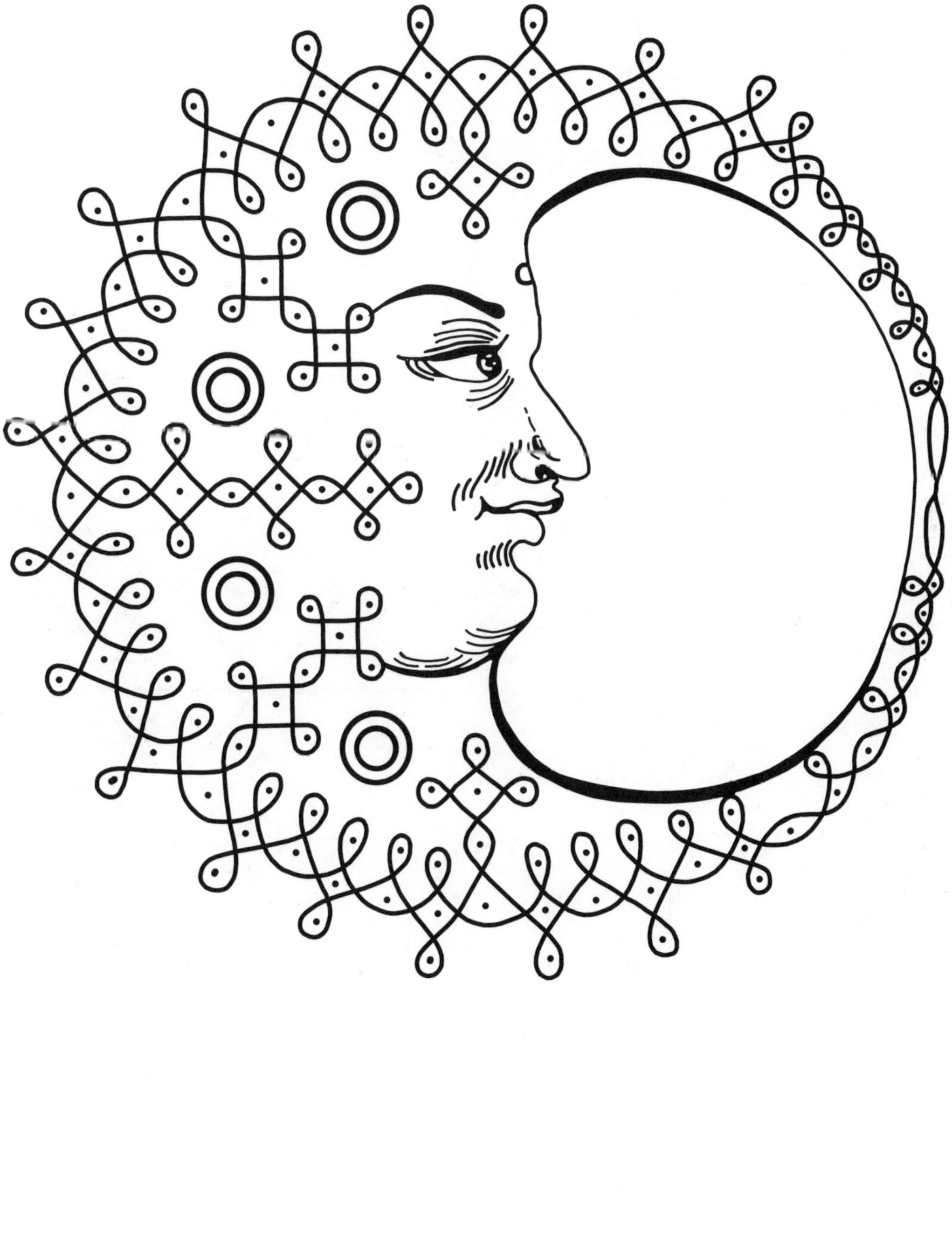



Moon

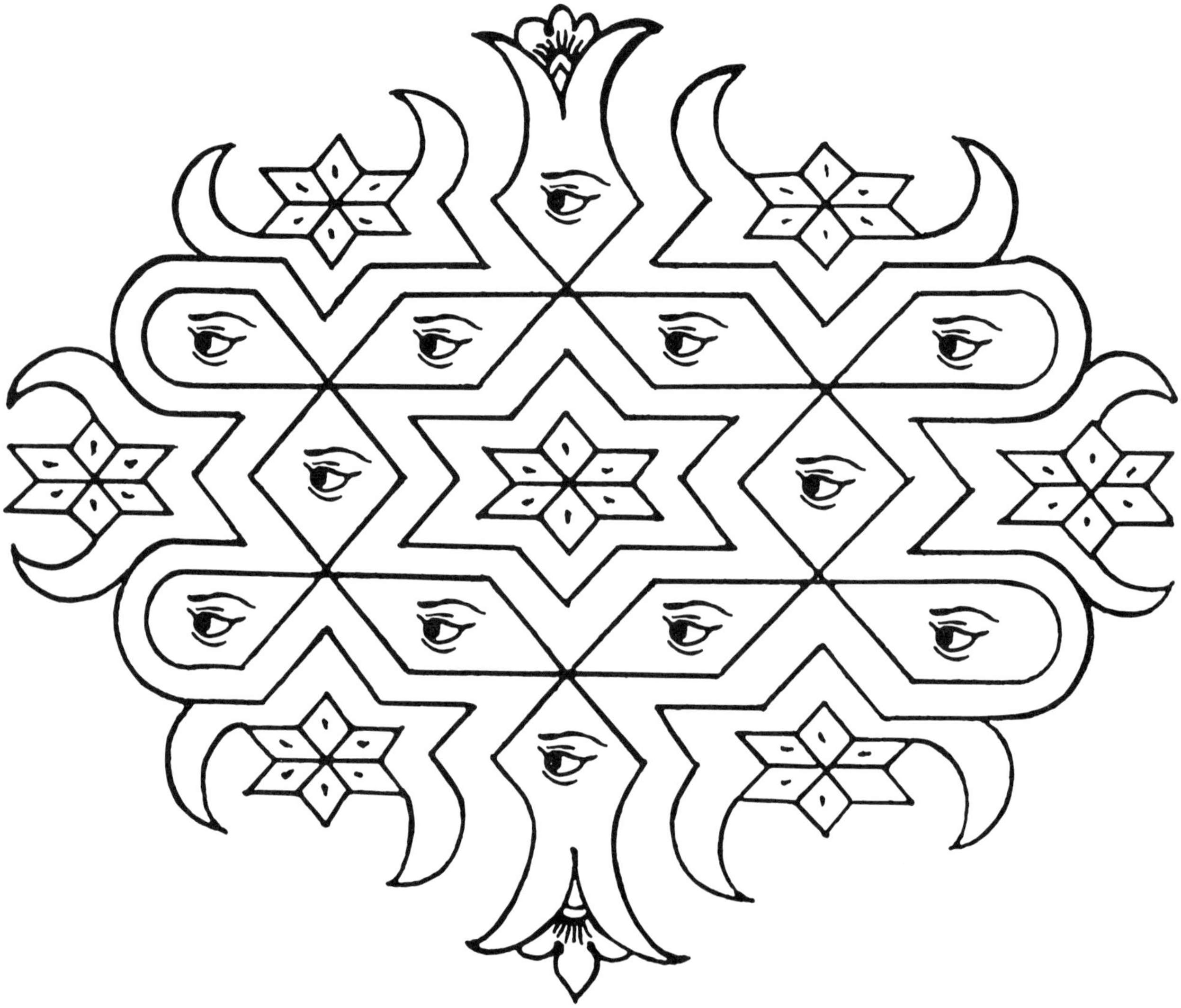

Eye of Indra

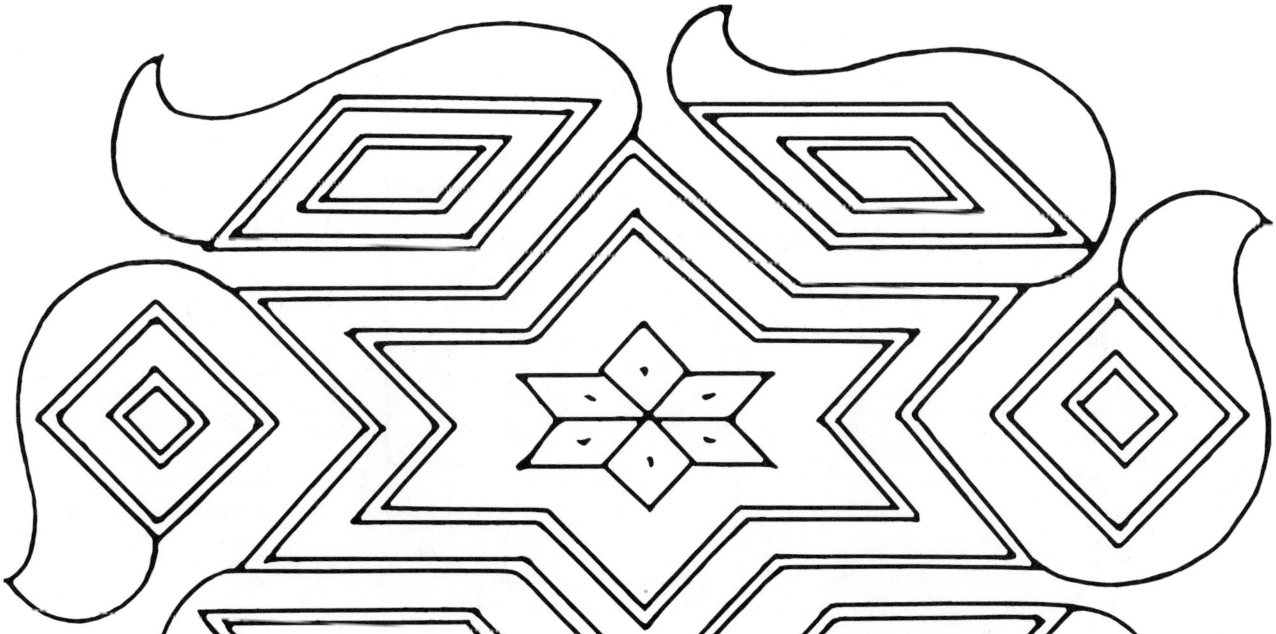

Beak of a peacock

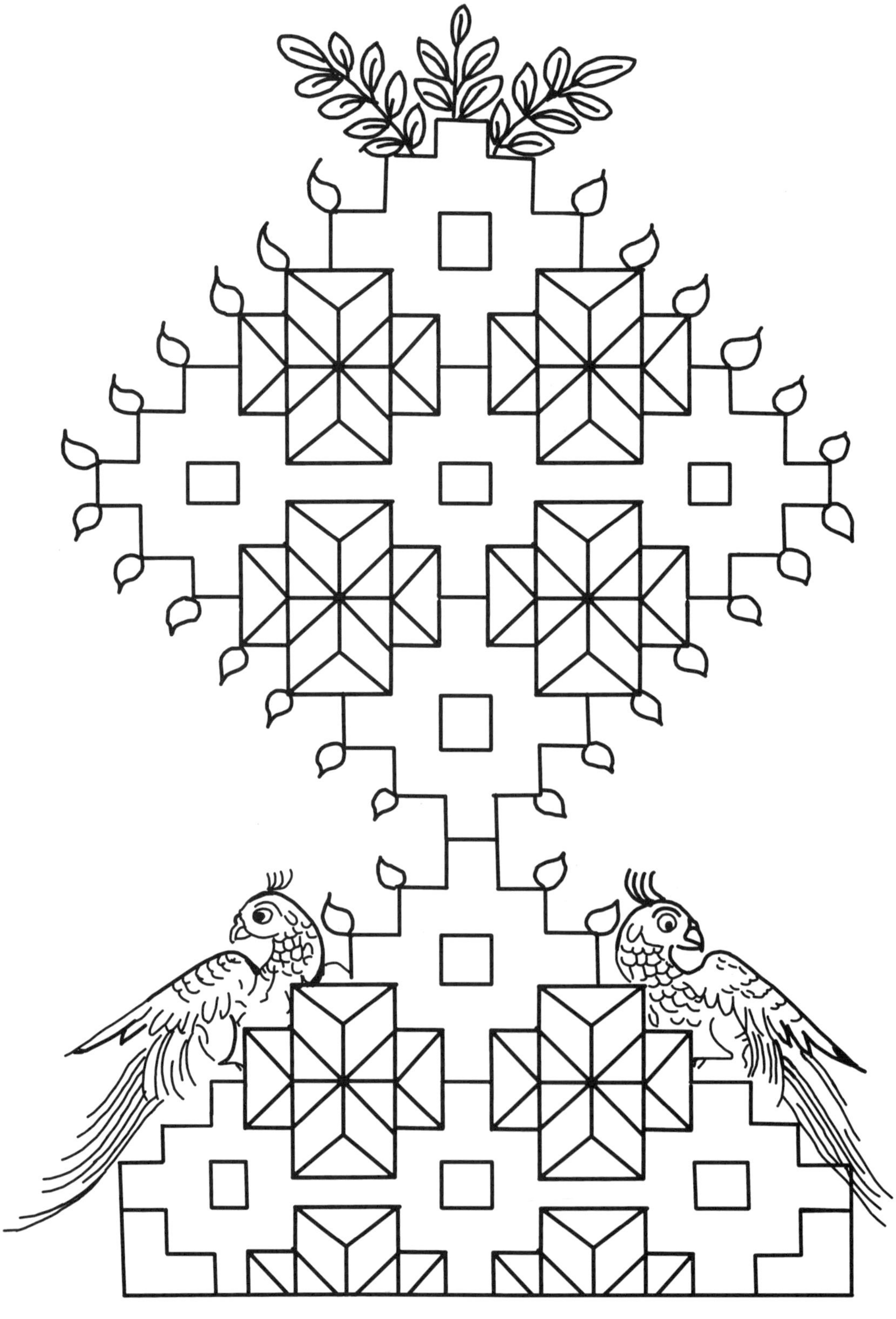



Tulasi altar

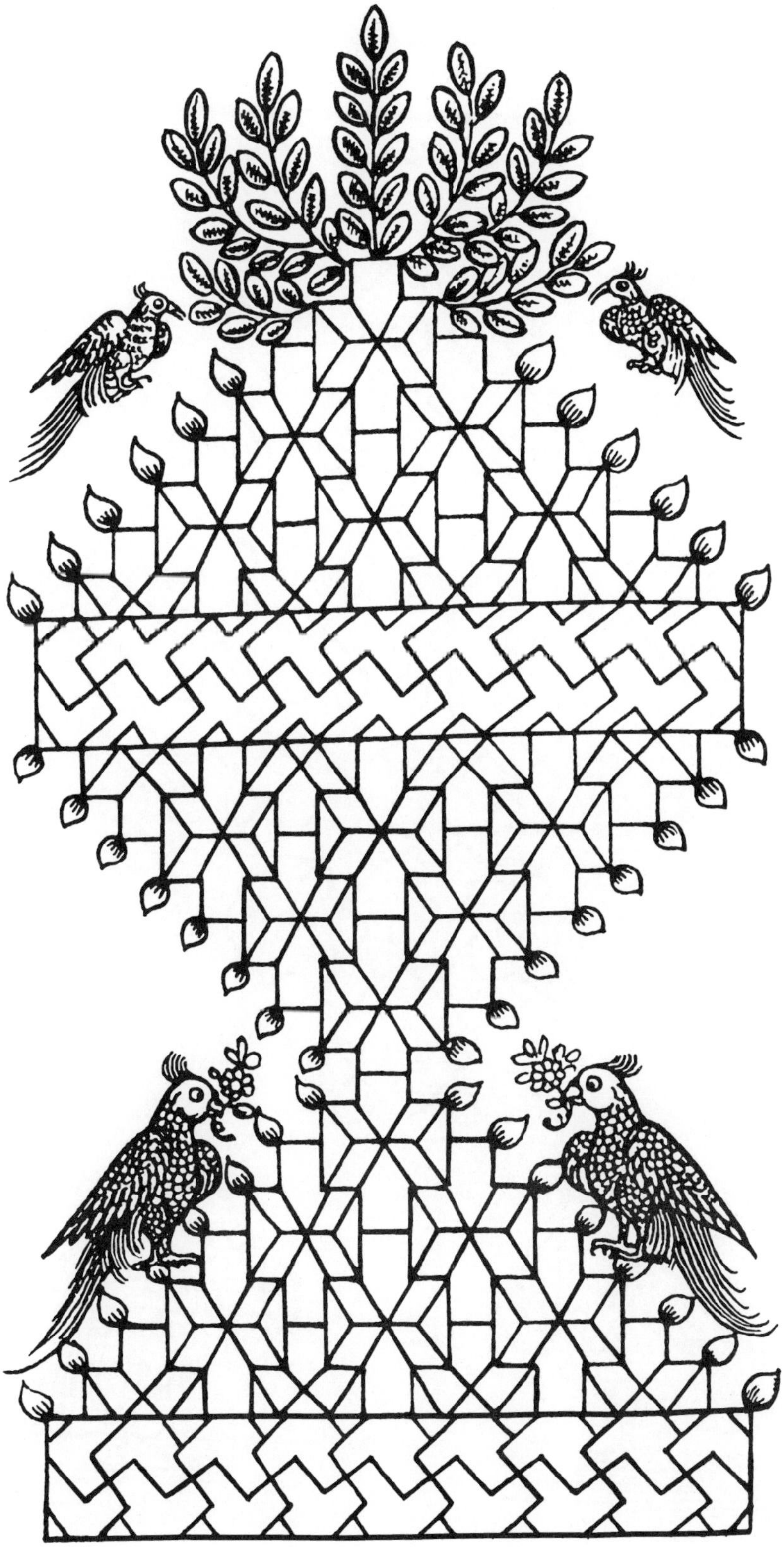



Garden of Krishna

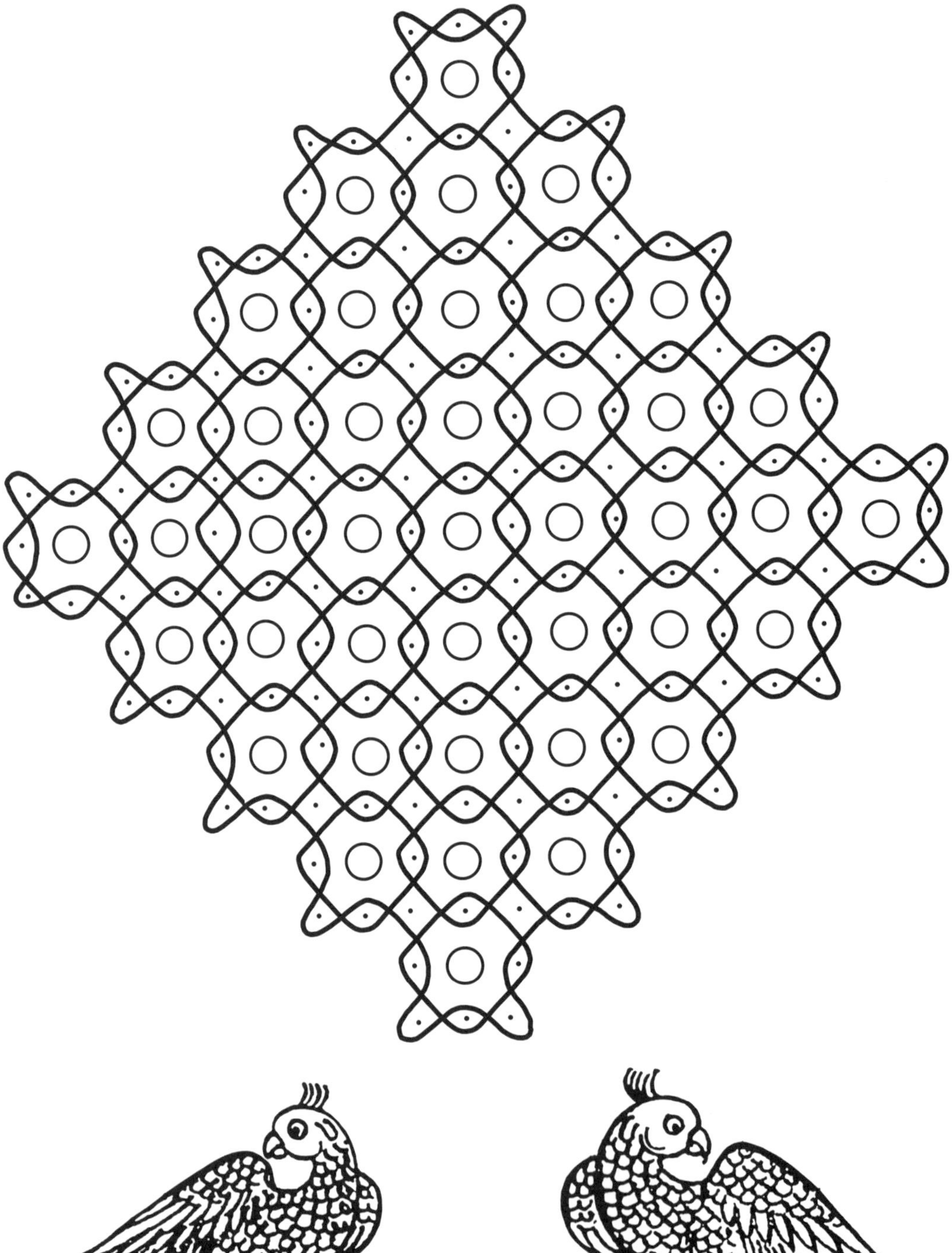

Talisman

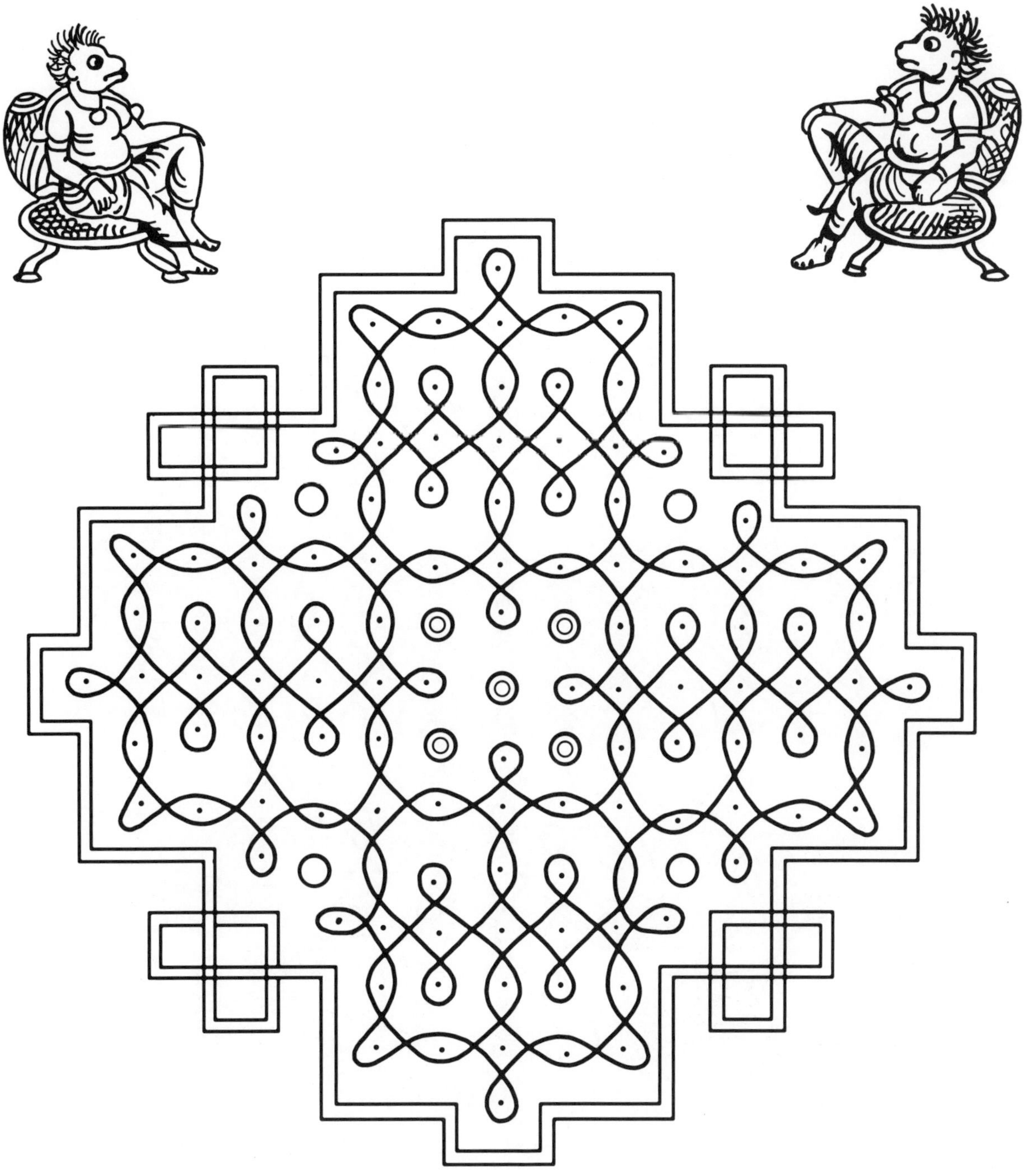

Wedding altar

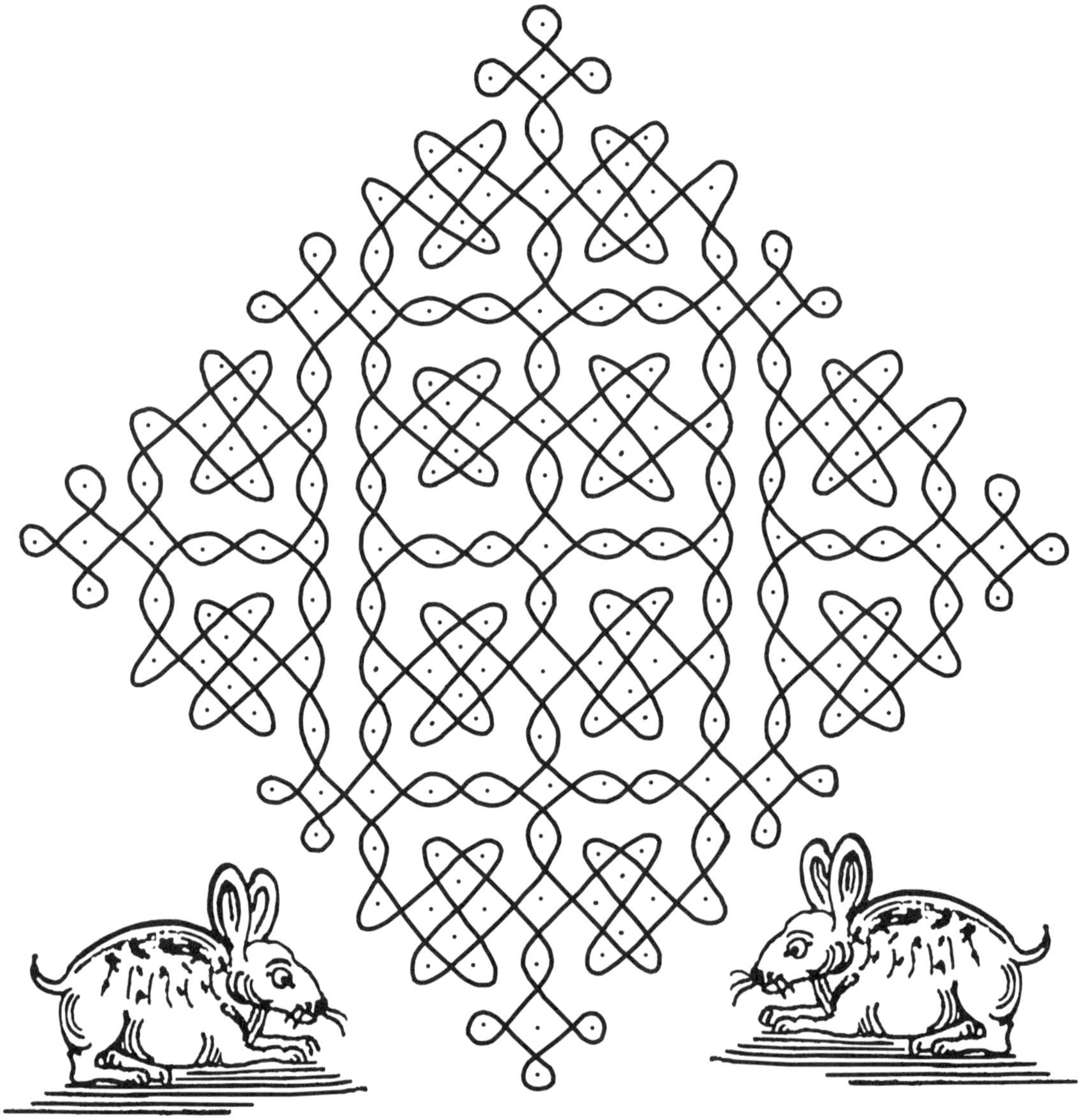

Bundle of sweets

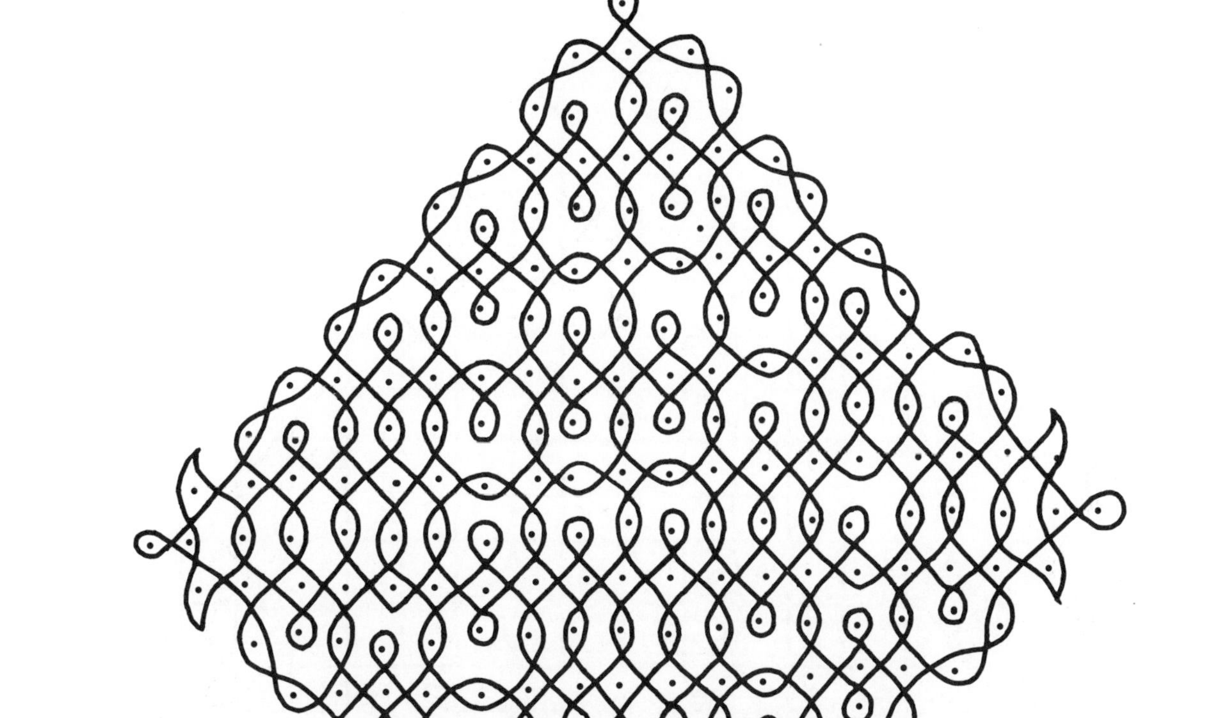



Brahma's hair

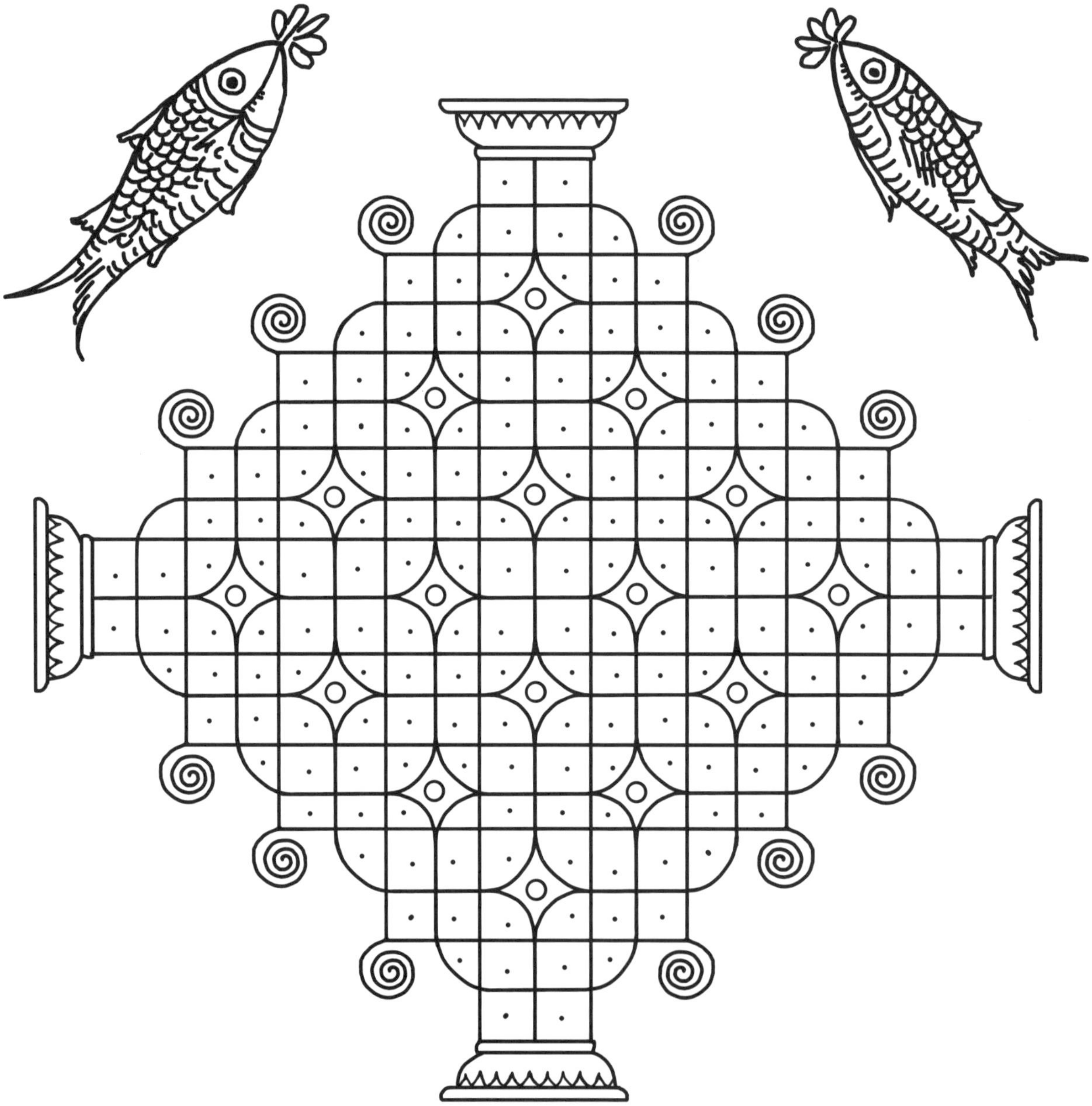



Wedding altar

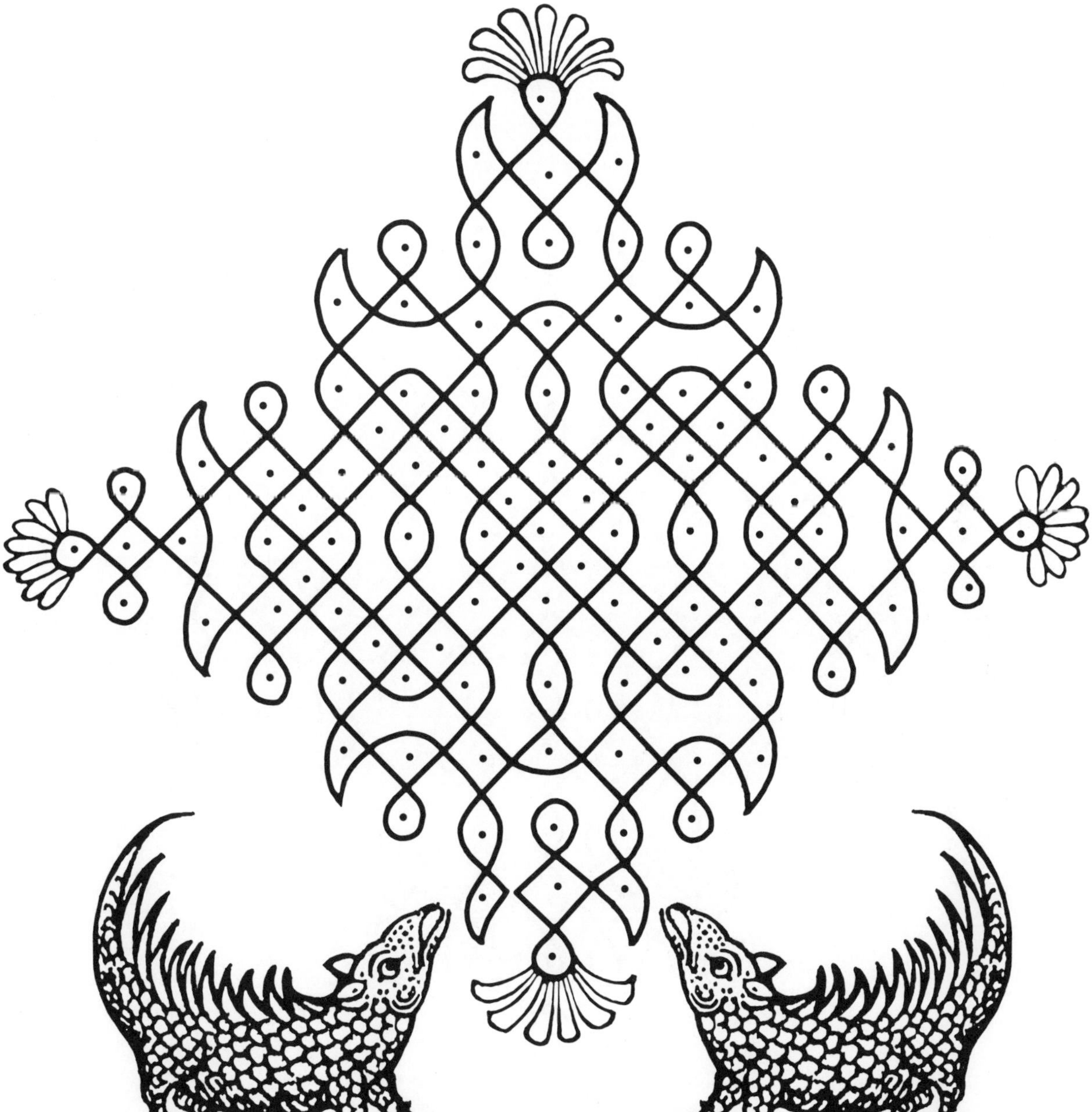



Scissors

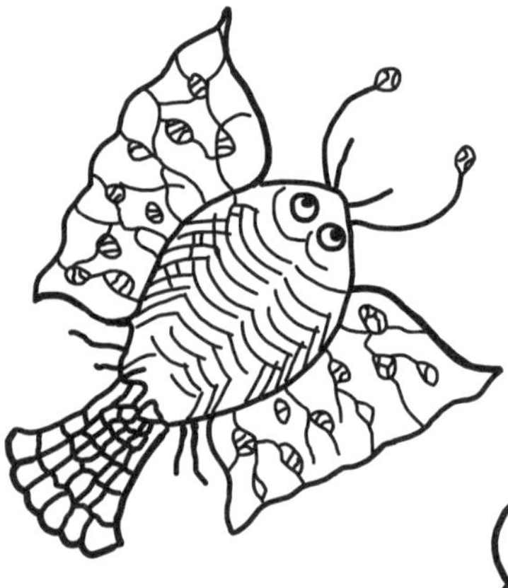
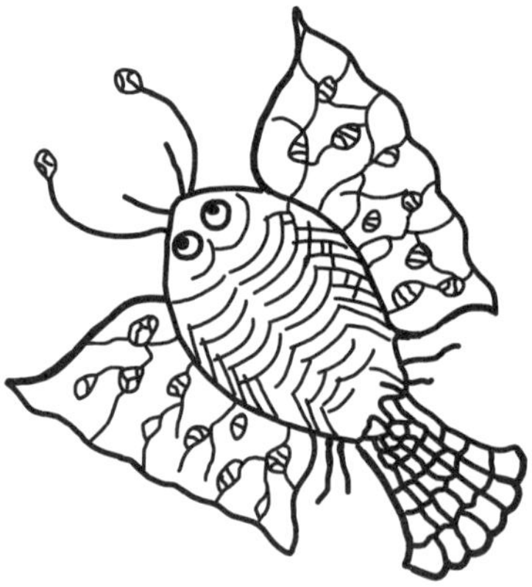
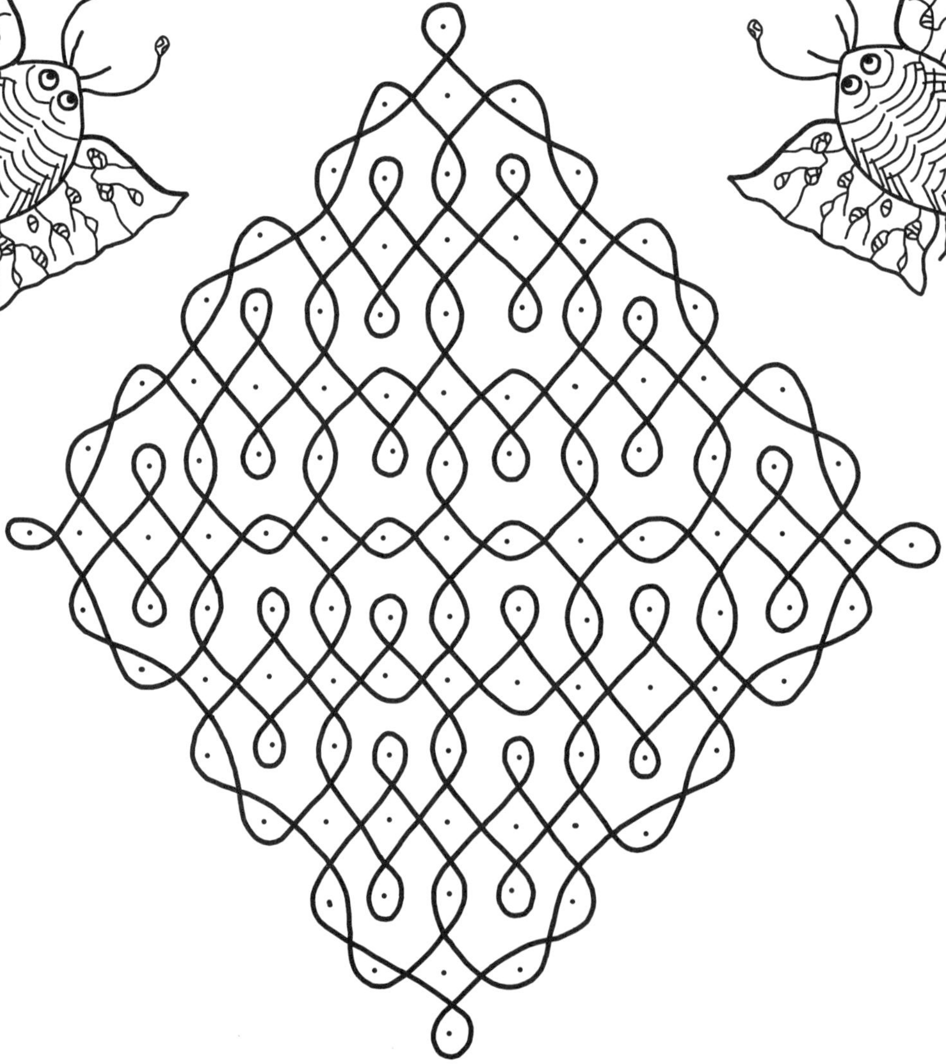



Brahma's hair

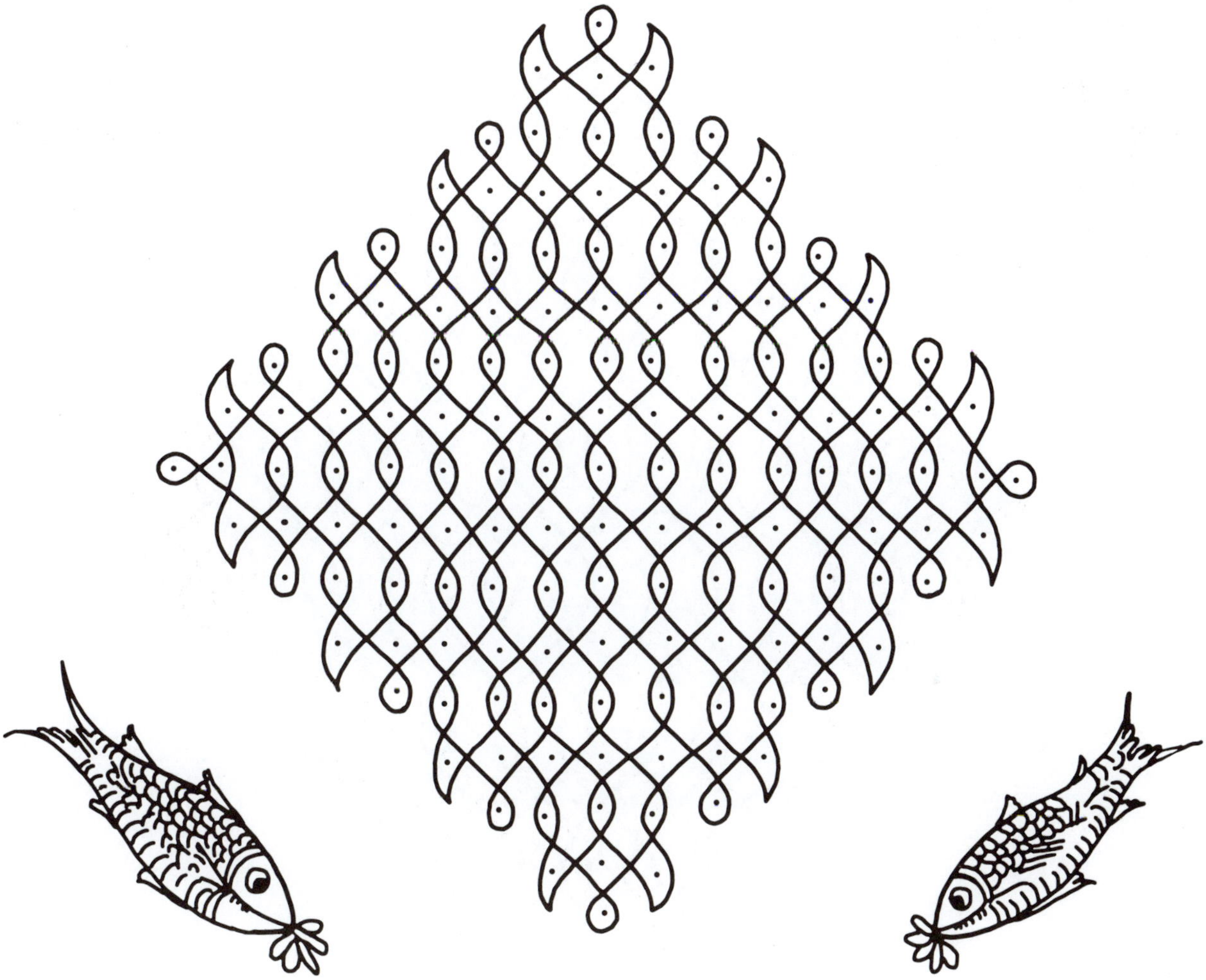



Scissors

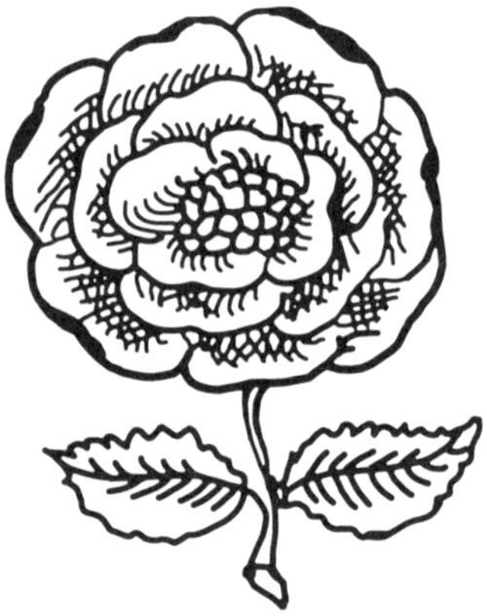

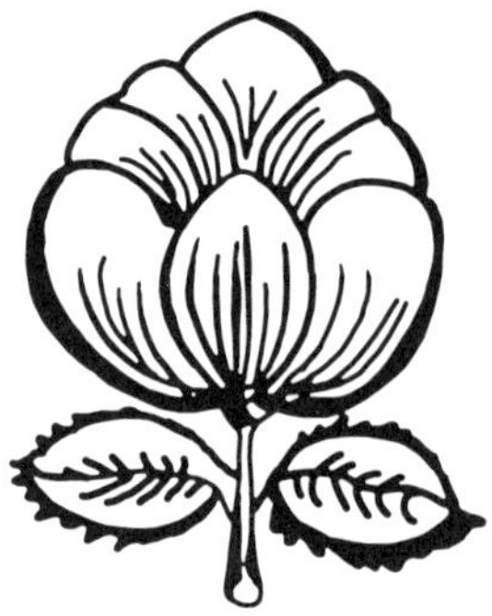

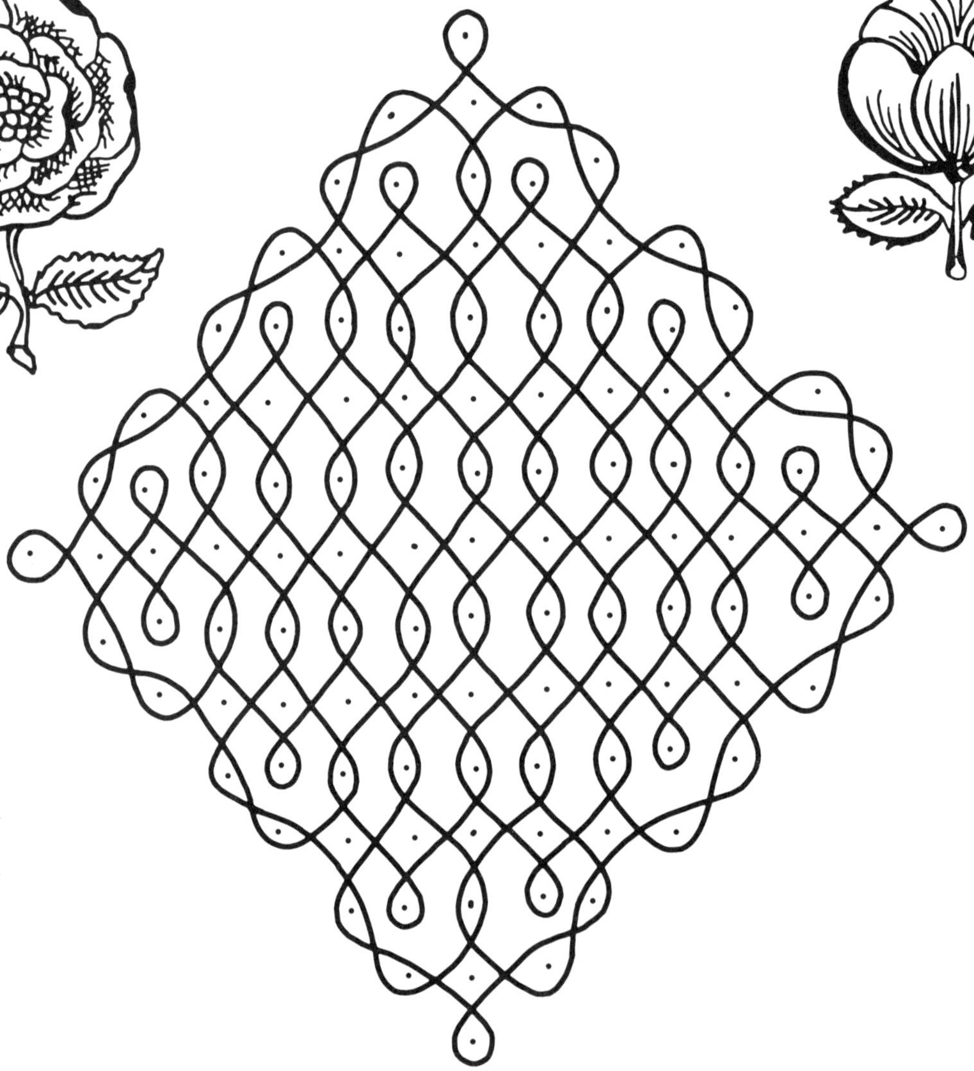



Brahma’s hair

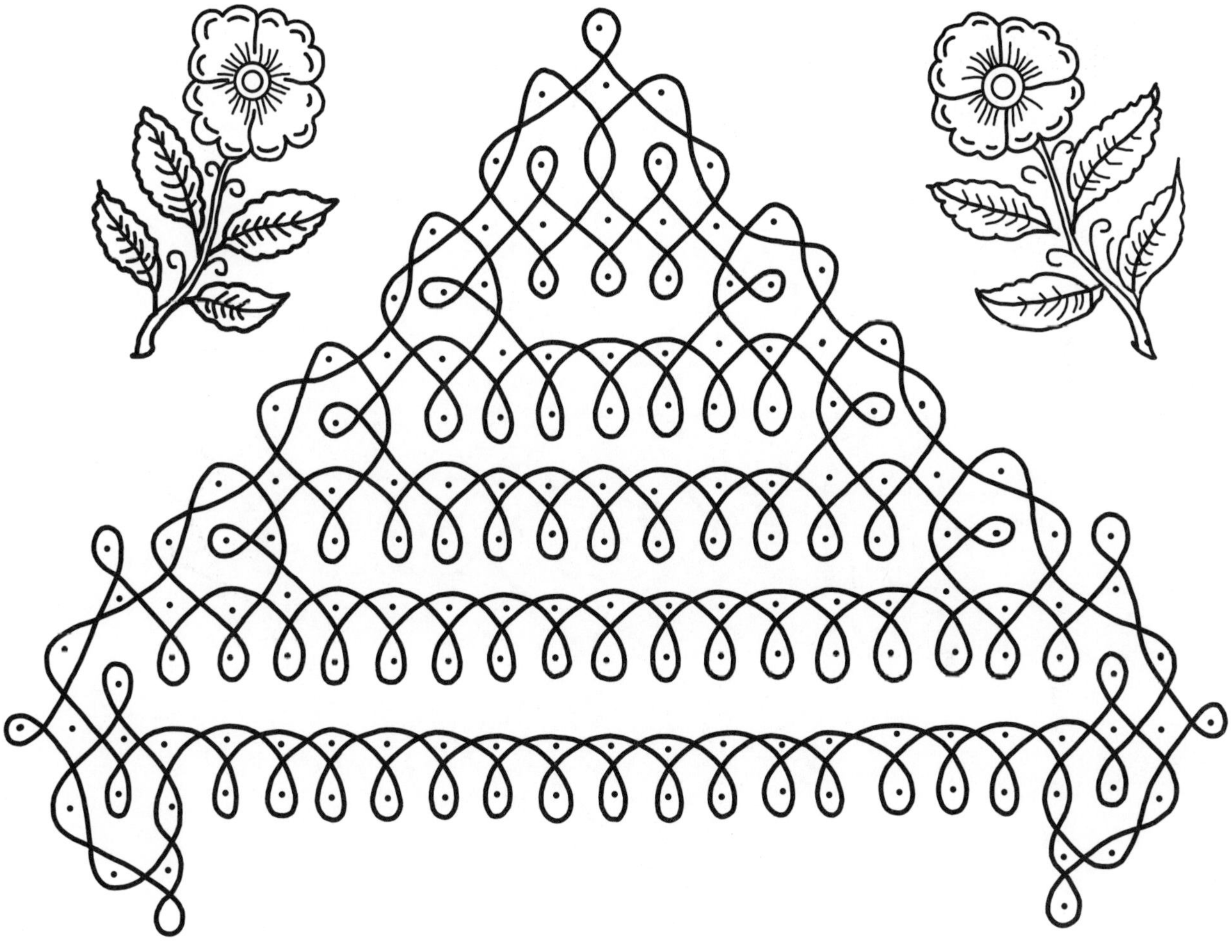



Crown

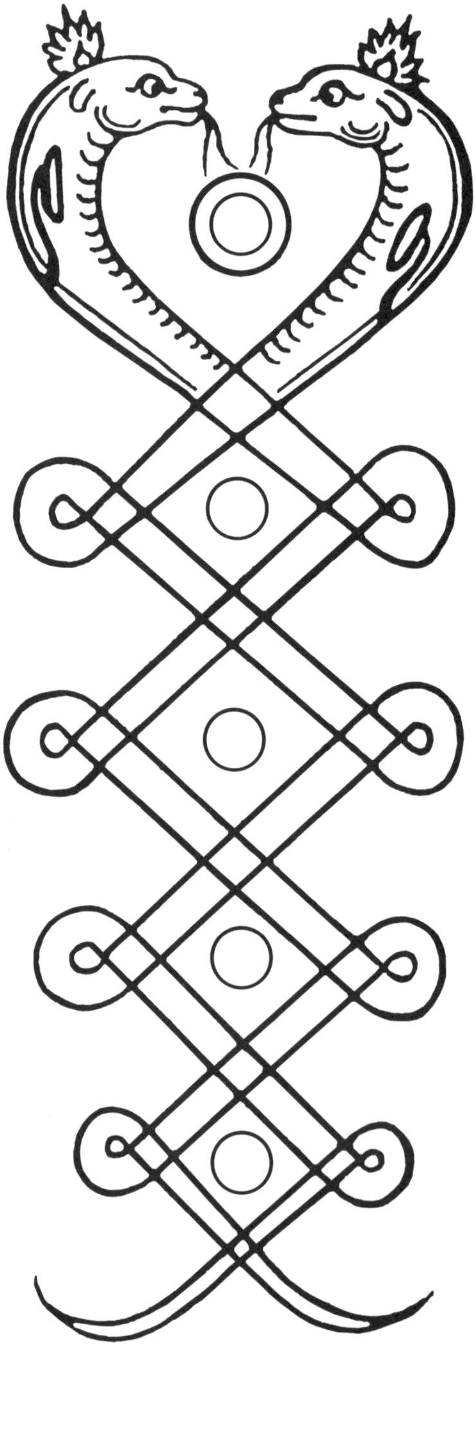



Double cobra

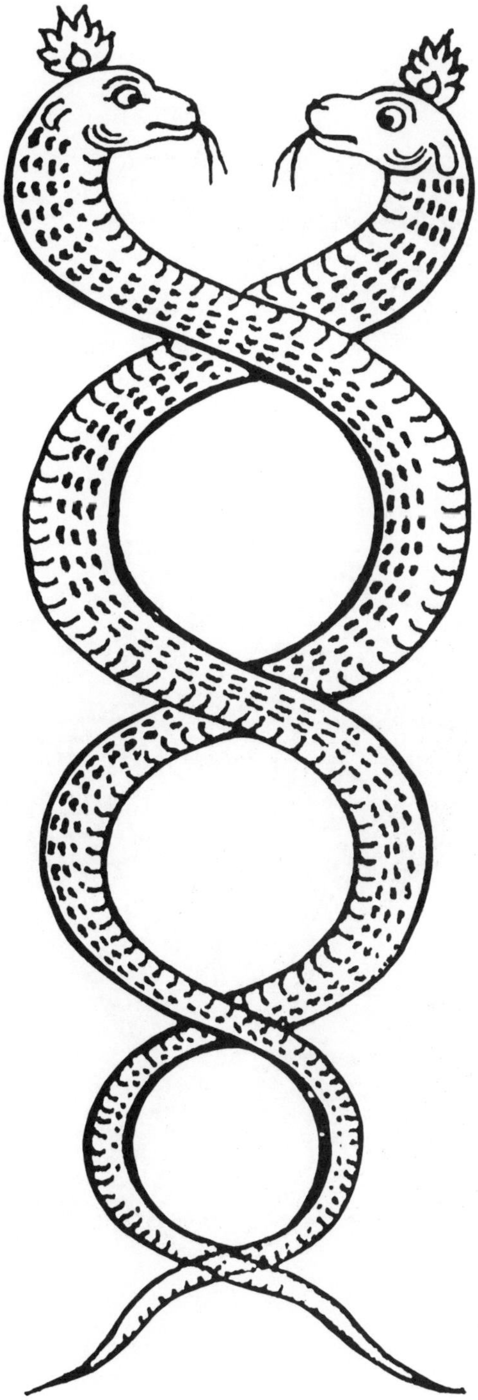



Pair of intertwined snakes

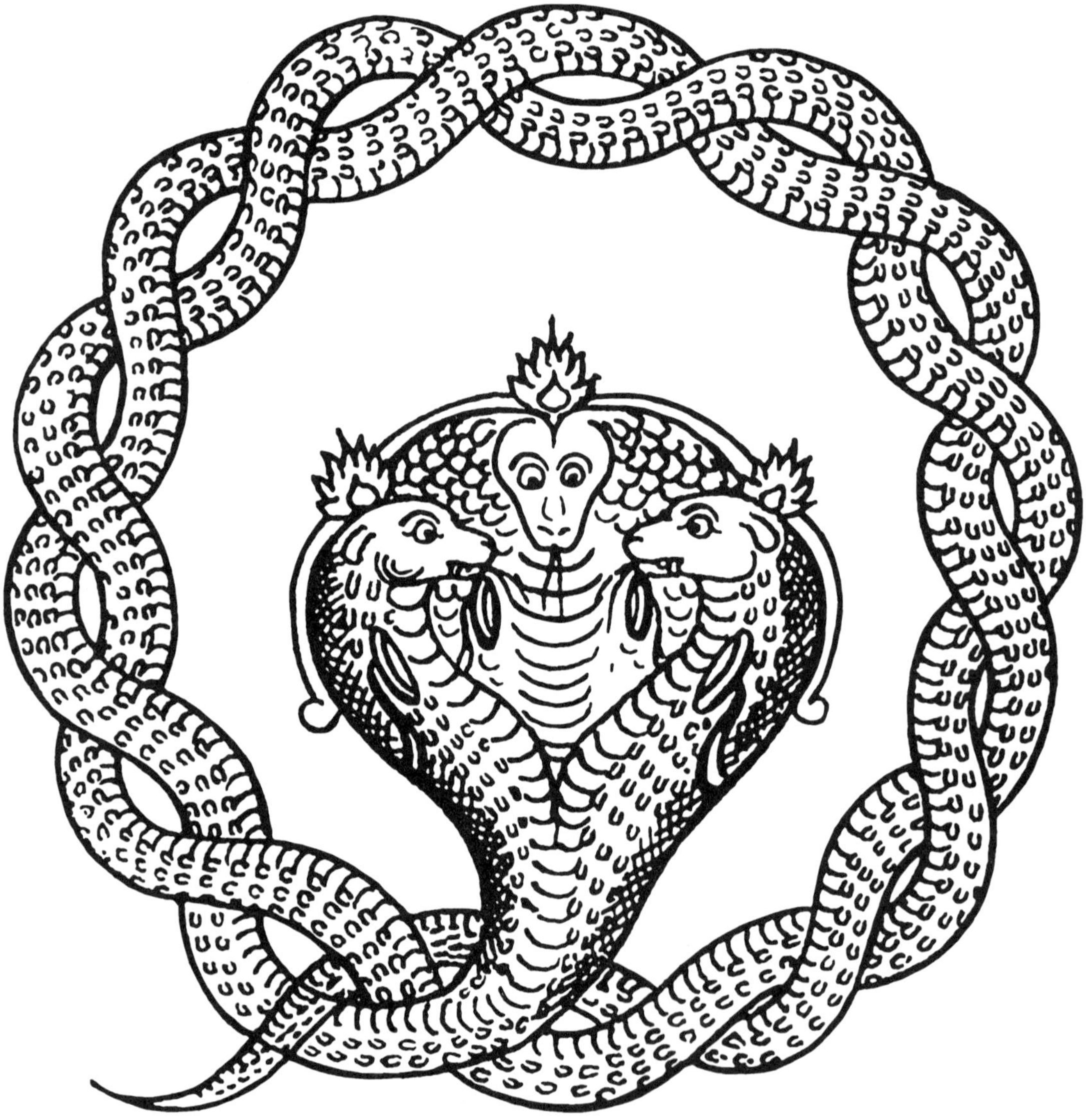

Knot of a single cobra

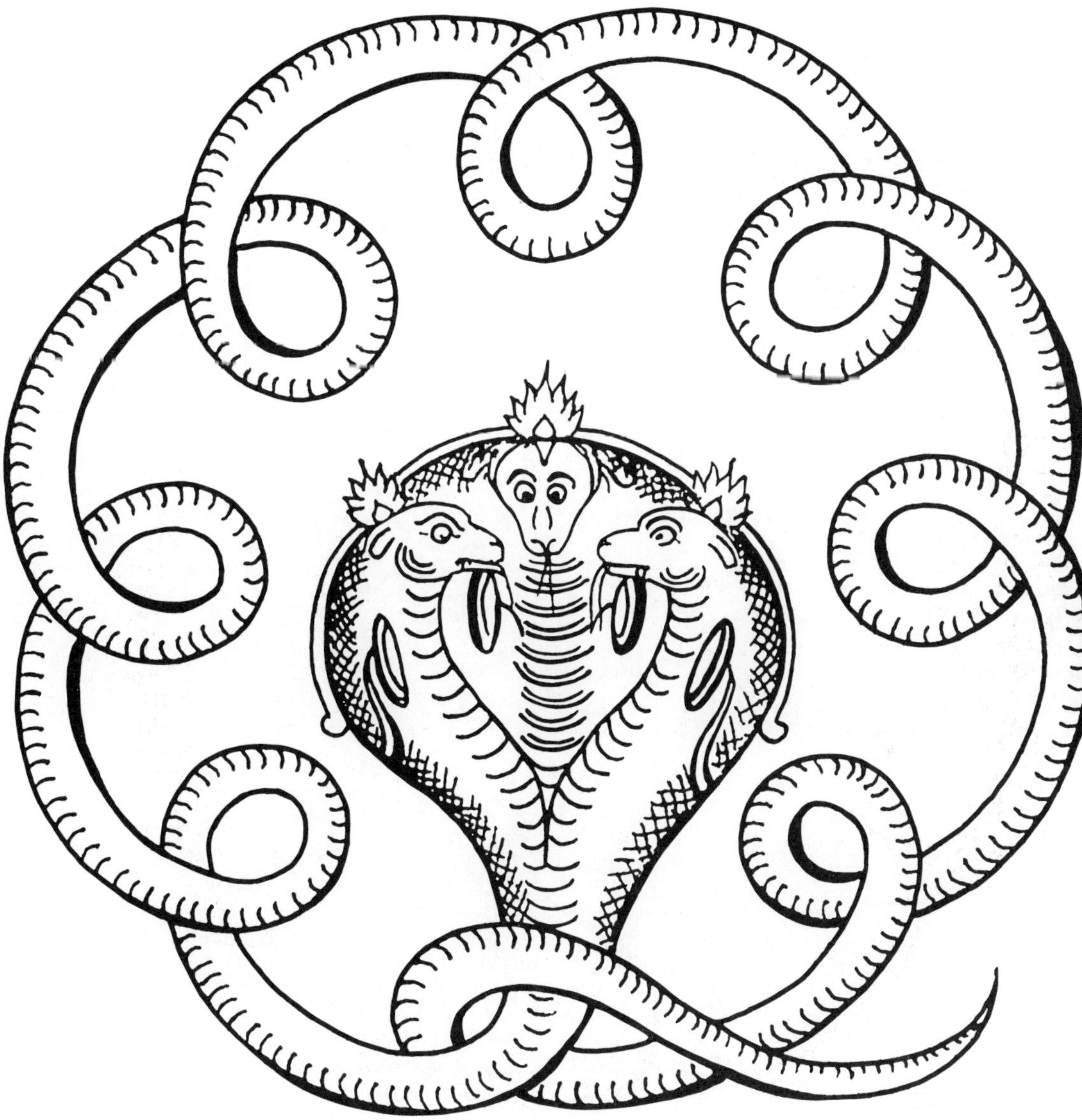



Knot of a single cobra

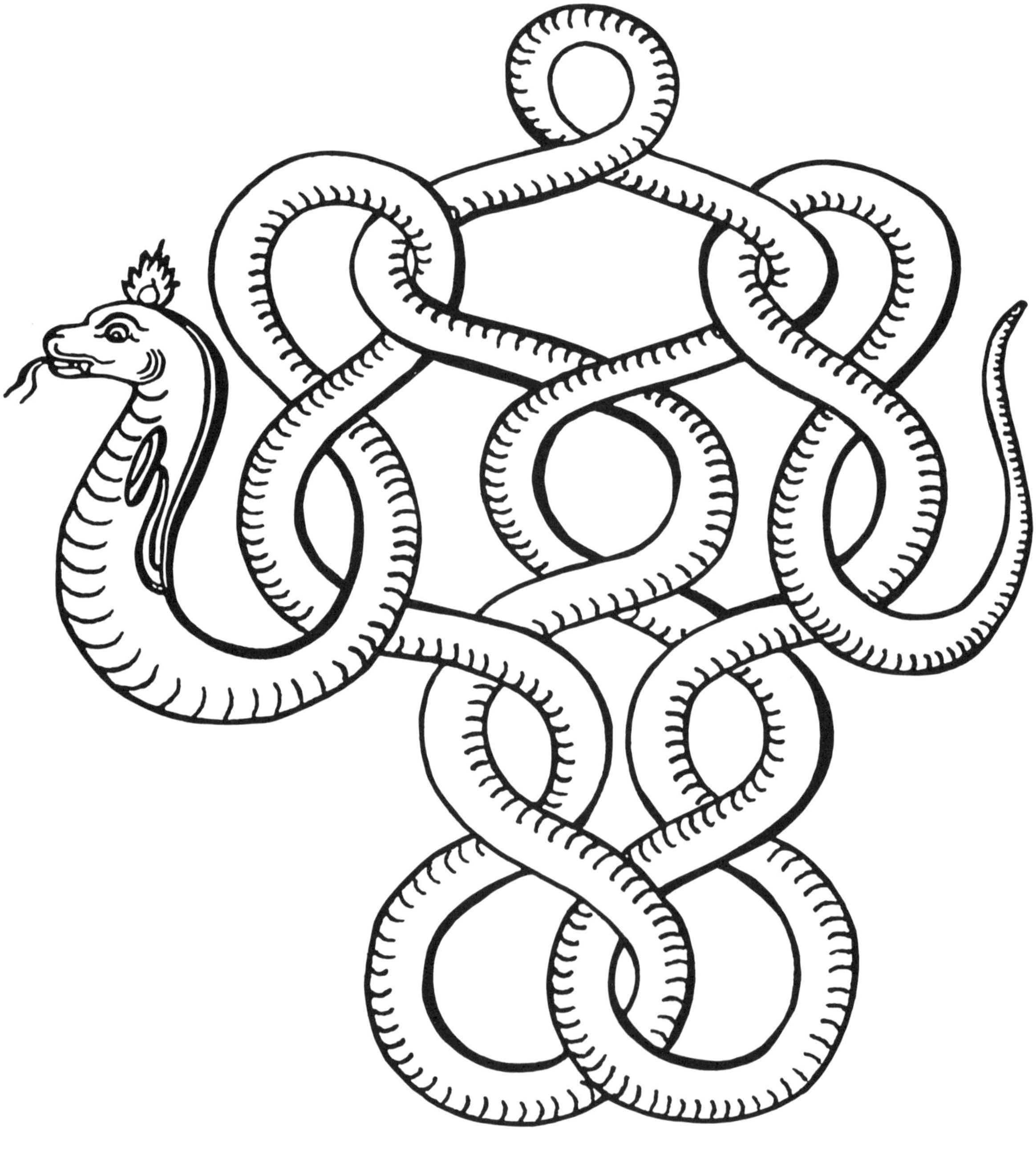

Knot of a single cobra

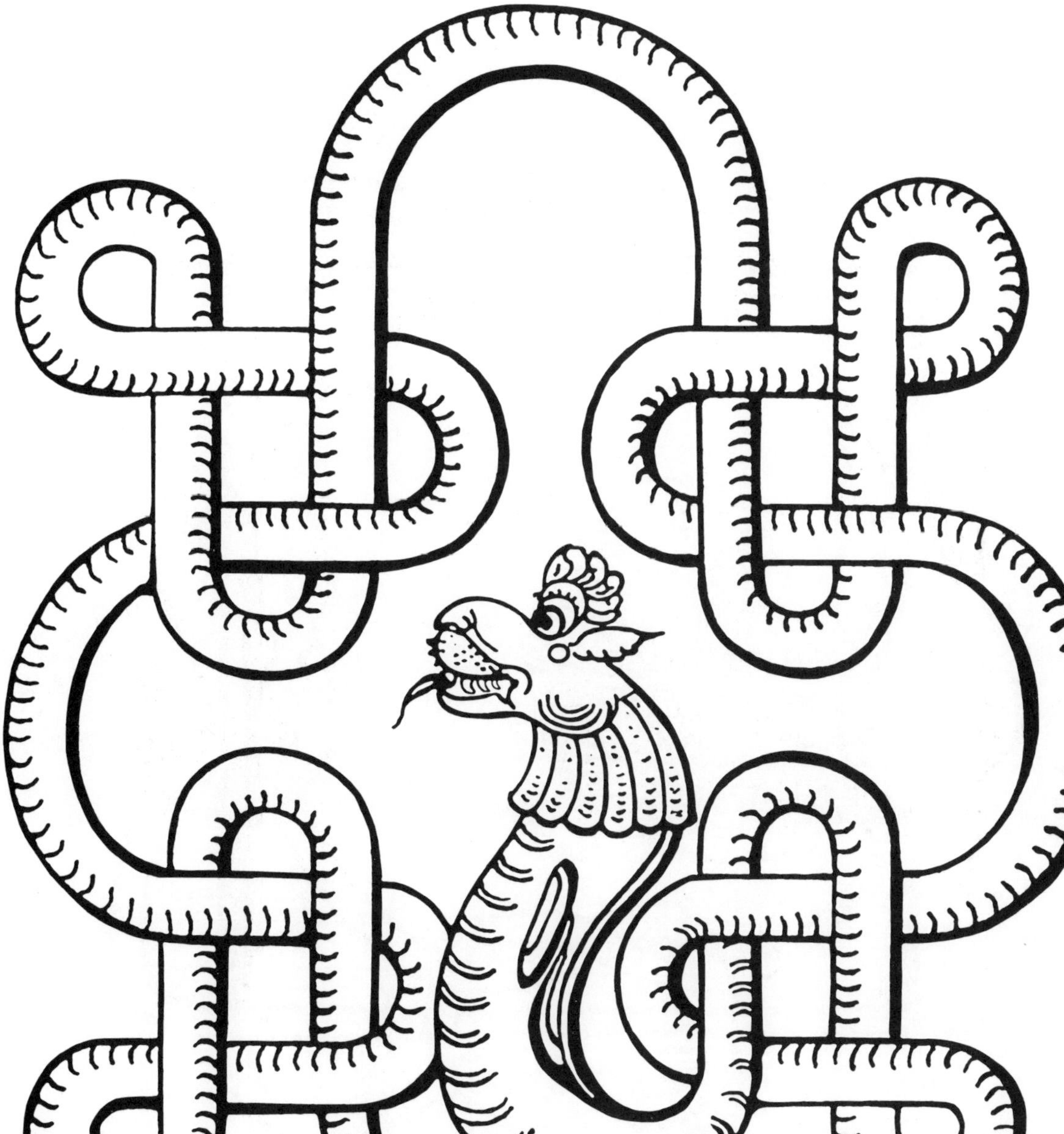



Knot of a Yali (mythological snake)

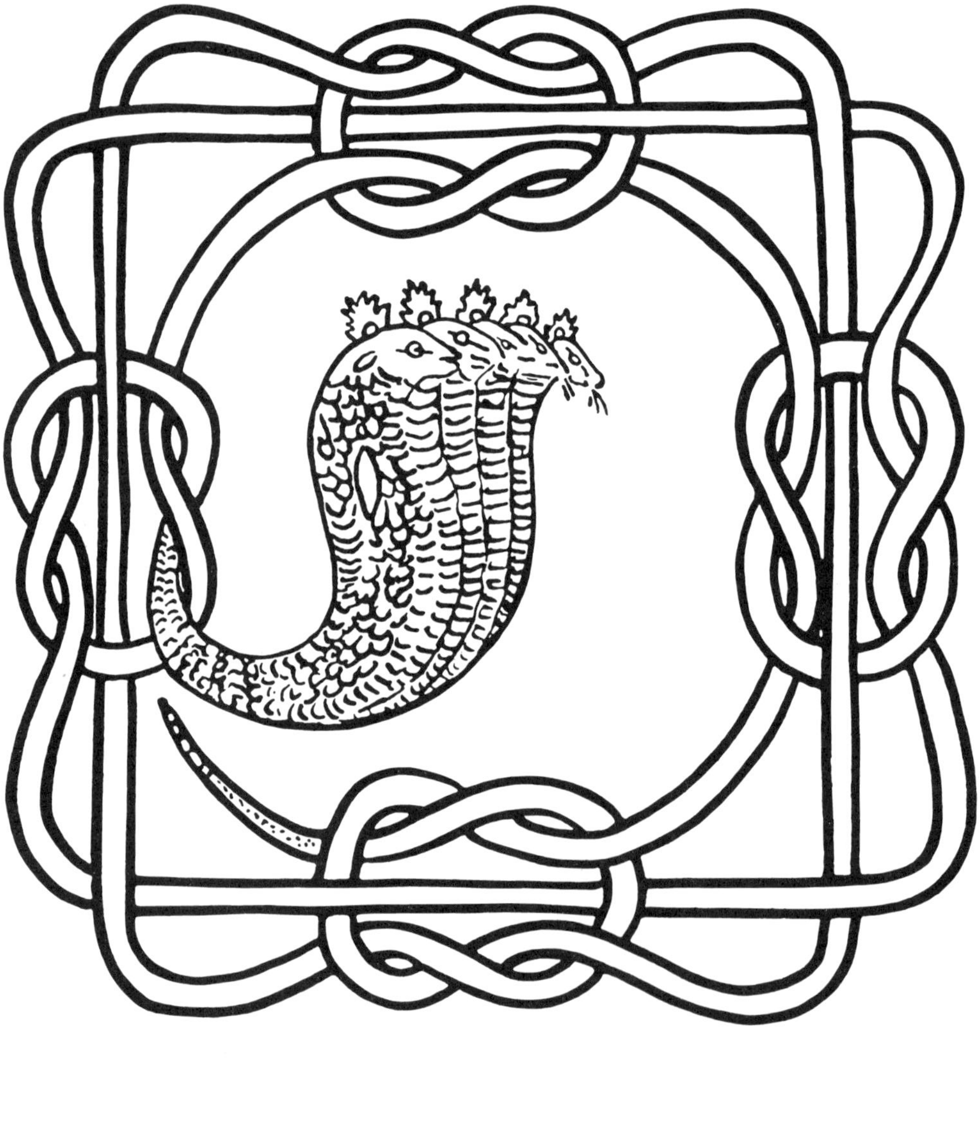

Border of a single cobra

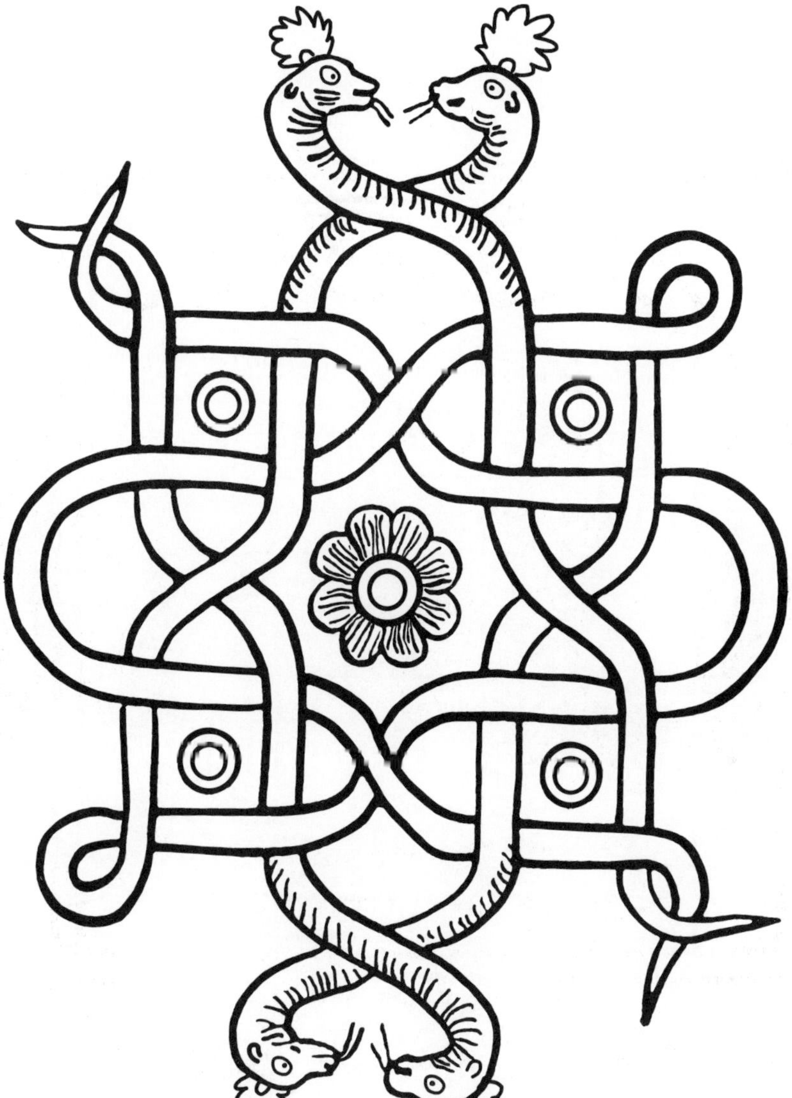



4 Intertwined cobra’s

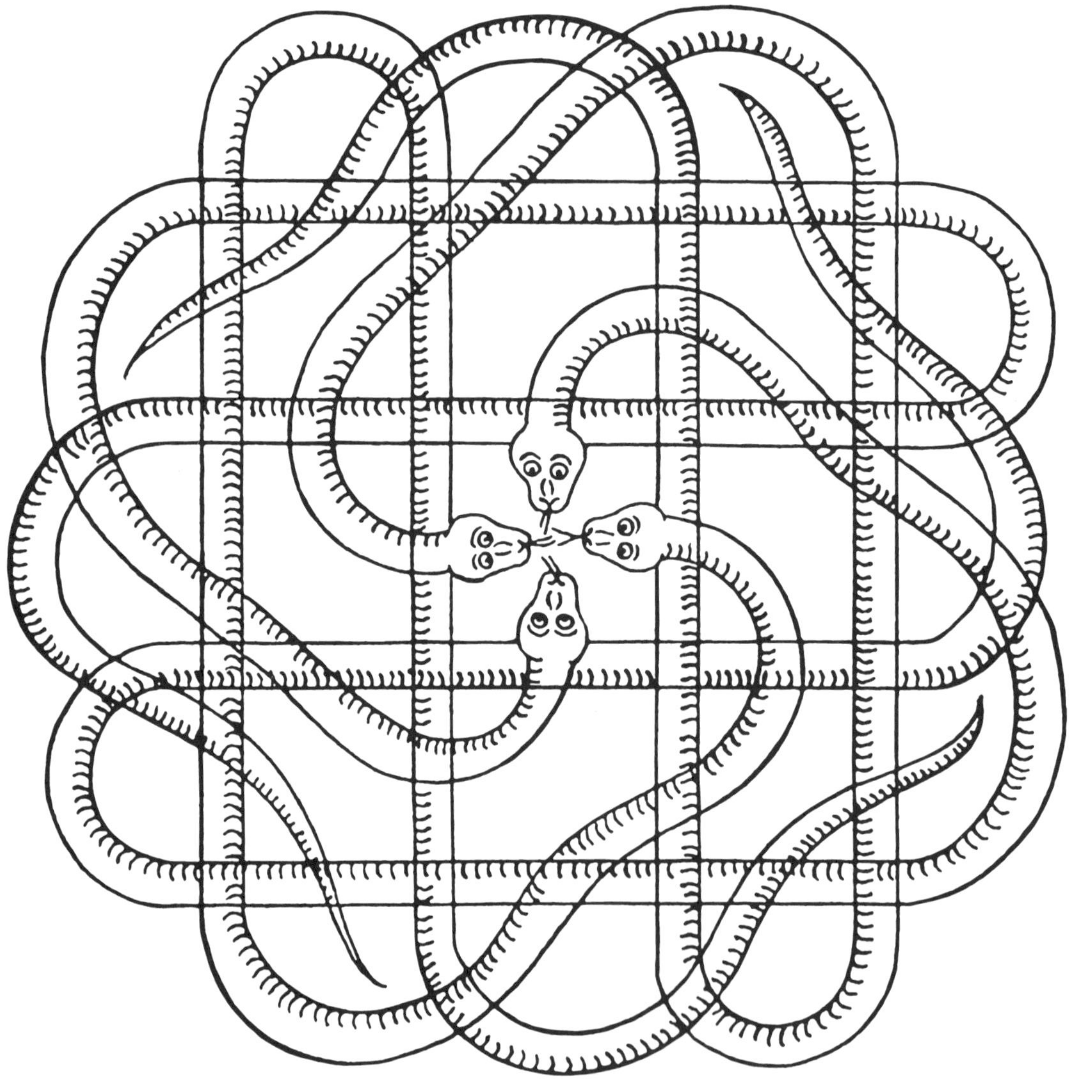



4 Facing intertwined snakes

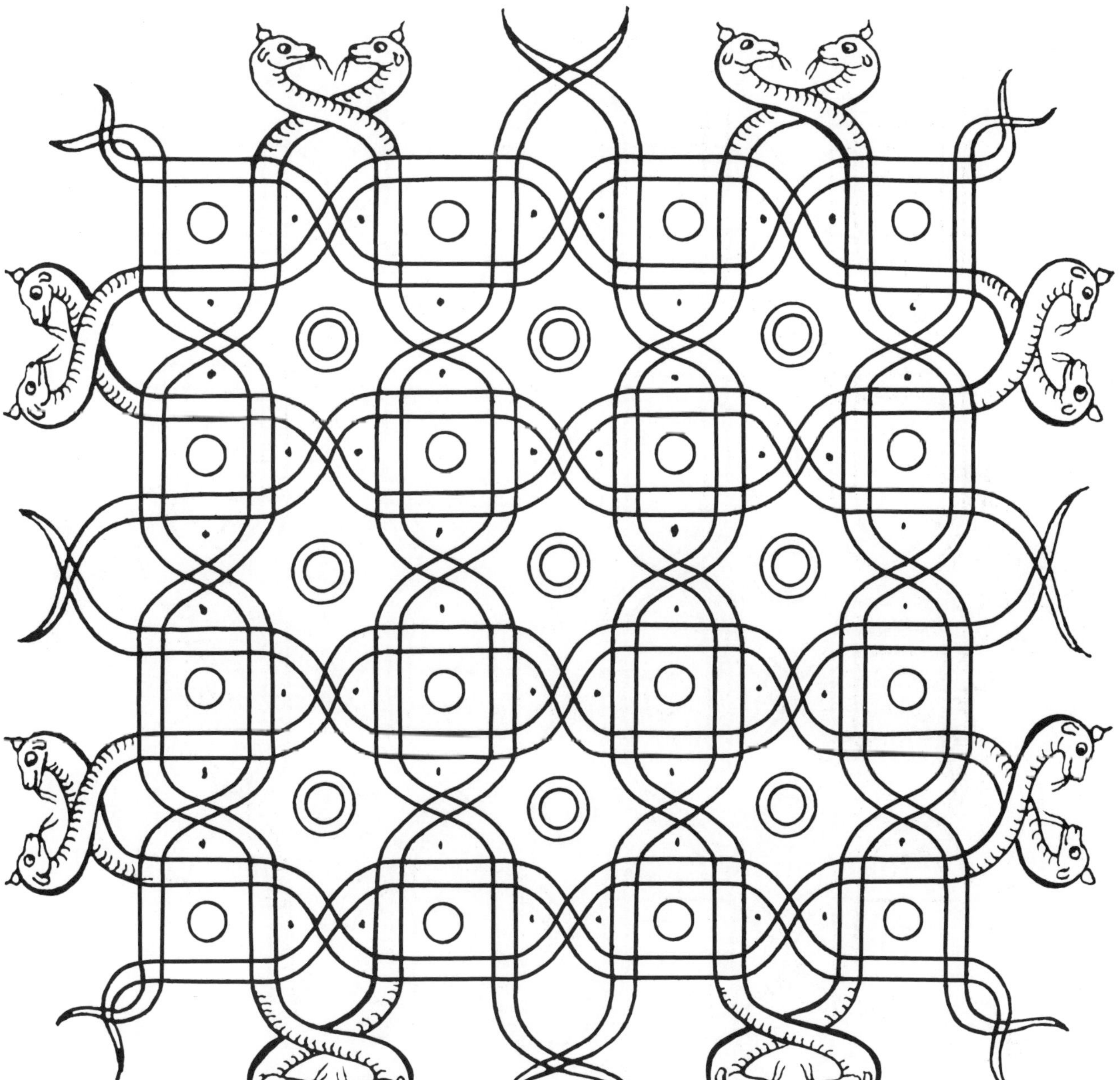

16 Intertwined cobra's

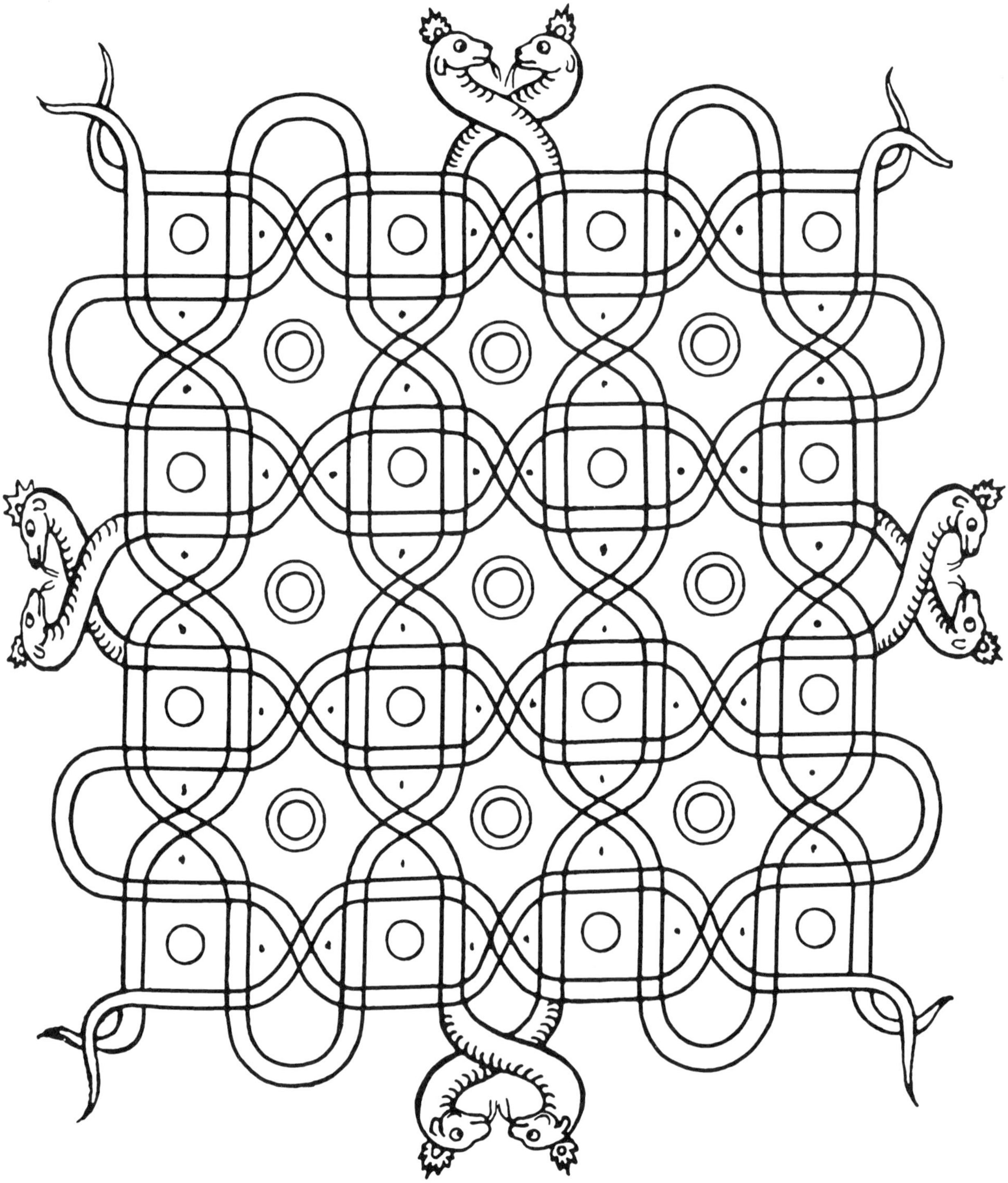

8 Intertwined cobra's

# INDEX

| P | English | Es | Français | Deutsch | Italiano |
|---|---|---|---|---|---|
| 55 | Cradle | Cun | Berceau | Wiege | Culla |
| 56 | Nose jewel | Nariz | Bijou nasal | Nasenschmuck | Gioiello da naso |
| 57 | Nose jewel | Nariz | ijou nasal | Nasenschmuck | Gioiello da Naso |
| 58 | Flying chariot | Carru | har volant | Fliegender Wagen | Carrozza volante |
| 59 | Brahma's hair | Pelo | heveu de Brahmane | Brahma's Haar | Capelli di Brahma |
| 60 | Chariot of flowers | Carru | har de fleurs | Blumenwagen | Carrozza di fiori |
| 61 | Chariot | Carru | ar | Wagen | Carrozza |
| 62 | Bunch of lemons | Manoj | s de citrons | Zitronenbündel | Limoni |
| 63 | Bunch of pineapples | Mano | d'ananas | Ananasbündel | Ananas |
| 64 | Stream of water | Arroyo | urant d'eau | Wasserlauf | Corso d'acqua |
| 65 | Elephant's foot | Pata de | d d'éléphant | Elefantenfuß | Zampa d'elefante |
| 66 | Pantal | Pantal | | Pantal | Pantal |
| 67 | Angled pattern | Diseño a | | Abgewinkeltes Muster | Motivo angolare |
| 68 | Cradle | Cuna | | Wiege | Culla |
| 69 | Cradle | Cuna | | | Culla |
| 70 | Twin bird | Aves gemelas | Oiseaux ju | | Uccelli gemelli |
| 71 | Talisman | Talismán | Talisman | Talism | Talismano |
| 72 | Talisman | Talismán | Talisman | Talisman | Talismano |
| 73 | Lighthouse | Faro | Phare | Leuchtturm | Faro |
| 74 | Leaf with a pattern | Diseño de hoja | Feuille avec motif | Blatt mit Muster | Foglia con motivo |
| 75 | Tray with designs | Bandeja con diseños | Plateau décoré | Tablett mit Designs | Vassoio disegnato |
| 76 | Sun | Sol | Soleil | Sonne | Sole |
| 77 | Moon | Luna | Lune | Mond | Luna |
| 78 | Eye of Indra | El ojo de Indra | Oeil d'Indra | Indras Auge | Occhio di Indra |
| 79 | Beak of a peacock | Pico de pavo real | Bec de paon | Pfauenschnabel | Becco di pavone |
| 80 | Tulasi altar | Altar Tulasi | Autel Tulasi | Tulasi Altar | Altare Tulasi |
| 81 | Garden of Krishna | El jardín de Krish | Jardin de Krishna | Krishnas Garten | Giardino di Krishna |
| 82 | Talisman | Talismán | man | Talisman | Talismano |
| 83 | Wedding altar | El altar de boda | riages | Hochzeitsaltar | Altare matrimoniale |
| 84 | Bundle of sweets | Fardo dulce | ies | Süßigkeiten | Fascio di dolci |
| 85 | Brahma's hair | Pelo de Brahm | | Brahmas Haar | Capelli di Brahma |
| 86 | Wedding altar | Altar de bod | | Hochzeitsaltar | Altare matrimoniale |
| 87 | Scissors | Tijeras | aux | | Forbici |
| 88 | Brahma's hair | Pelo de Brahma | Cheveu de Brahmane | Brahmas Haar | Capelli di Brahma |
| 89 | Scissors | Tijeras | Ciseaux | Scheren | Forbici |
| 90 | Brahma's hair | Pelo de Brahma | Cheveu de Brahmane | Brahmas Haar | Capelli di Brahma |
| 91 | Crown | Corona | Couronne | Krone | Corona |
| 92 | Double cobra | Cobra doble | Double cobra | Doppelkobra | Cobra doppio |
| 93 | Pair of intertwined snakes | Serpientes entrelazada | Couple de serpents entrelacés | Paar verschlungener Schlangen | Coppia di serpenti intrecciati |
| 94 | Knot of a single cobra | Nudo de una única cobra | Noeud d'un seul cobra | Knoten einer Einzelkobra | Nodo formato da un cobra |
| 95 | Knot of a single cobra | Nudo de una única cobra | Noeud d'un seul cobra | Knoten einer Einzelkobra | Nodo formato da un cobra |
| 96 | Knot of a single cobra | Nudo de una única cobra | Noeud d'un seul cobra | Knoten einer Einzelkobra | Nodo formato da un cobra |
| 97 | Knot of a Yali (mythological snake) | Nudo de Yali (serpiente mitológica) | Nœud de Yali ( serpent mythologique) | Yali Knoten (Schlange der Mythologie) | Nodo formato da uno Yali (serpente mitologico) |
| 98 | Border of a single cobra | Borde de una única cobra | Bord d'un seul cobra | Schmuckleiste einer Kobra | Contorno di un cobra |
| 99 | 4 Intertwined cobras | 4 Interrelación de cobras | 4 Cobras entrelacés | 4 Verschlungene Kobras | Quattro cobra intrecciati |
| 100 | 4 Facing intertwined snakes | 4 Encarado hacia las serpi-entes entrelazadas | 4 Serpents entrelacés face à face | 4 Gegenüberstehende verschlungene Kobras | Quattro cobra intrecciati che si guardano |
| 101 | 16 Intertwined cobras | 16 Cobras entrelazadas | 16 Cobras entrelacés | 16 Verschlungene Kobras | Sedici cobra intrecciati |
| 102 | 8 Intertwined cobras | 8 Cobras entrelazadas | 8 Cobras entrelacés | 8 Verschlungene Kobras | Otto cobra intrecciati |